A CHILD IN THE HOLY LAND

A CHILD IN THE HOLY LAND

Compiled and Edited by
GISU MOHADJER

BAHÁ'Í
PUBLISHING
WILMETTE, ILLINOIS

Bahá'í Publishing, Wilmette, Illinois
1233 Central St, Evanston, Illinois 60201
Copyright © 2022 by Gisu Mohadjer
All rights reserved. Published 2022
Printed in the United States of America ∞
25   24   23   22   1   2   3   4

Library of Congress Cataloging-in-Publication Data

Names: Mohadjer, Gisu, compiler, editor.
Title: A child in the Holy Land / compiled and edited by
    Gisu Mohadjer.
Description: Wilmette, Illinois : Bahá'í Publishing, [2022] |
    Includes bibliographical references and index.
Identifiers: LCCN 2022026484 (print) | LCCN 2022026485
    (ebook) | ISBN
    9781618512178 (paperback) | ISBN 9781618512185 (epub)
Subjects: LCSH: Bahais--Biography. | Bahá'u'lláh, 1817-1892. |
    'Abdu'l-Bahá, 1844-1921. | Shoghi, Effend.i
Classification: LCC BP390 .M66 2022 (print) | LCC BP390
    (ebook) | DDC 297.9/3092 [B]--dc23/eng/20220711
LC record available at https://lccn.loc.gov/2022026484
LC ebook record available at https://lccn.loc.gov/2022026485

Cover photo by Farzam Sabetian
Cover design by Carlos Esparza
Book design by Patrick Falso

O Lord!

I am a child; enable me to grow beneath the shadow of Thy loving-kindness.

I am a tender plant; cause me to be nurtured through the outpourings of the clouds of Thy bounty.

I am a sapling of the garden of love; make me into a fruitful tree.

Thou art the Mighty and the Powerful, and Thou art the All-Loving, the All-Knowing, the All-Seeing.

'Abdu'l-Bahá

This book is dedicated to

Hand of the Cause of God Amatu'l-Bahá Rúḥíyyih <u>Kh</u>ánum
who made my childhood heavenly

And to my dear mother
Knight of Bahá'u'lláh Iran Furútan Muhájir
who first took me to the Holy Land
when I was a child of forty days

Hand of the Cause of God Amatu'l-Bahá Rúḥíyyih <u>Kh</u>ánum holding Gisu
as a baby, with Iran Furútan Muhájir standing in the back row second
from the left. This photograph was taken in the Haifa Pilgrim House in
1961.

Seated next to Hand of the Cause of God Amatu'l-Bahá Rúḥíyyih
<u>Kh</u>ánum is Ms. 'Aṭá'íyyih Furútan. Also standing in the back row from
left to right are: Dr. Luṭfu'lláh Ḥakím, Ms. Bahíyyih Ḥakím, and Mr. 'Alí
Na<u>kh</u>javání, and Hand of the Cause of God Ṭarázu'lláh Samandarí.

Contents

Acknowledgments xi

Publisher's Note xiii

Introduction xv

Stories with the Blessed Beauty Bahá'u'lláh 1

Stories with the Beloved Master 'Abdu'l-Bahá 19

Stories about Shoghi Effendi as a Child 59

Stories with the Beloved Guardian Shoghi Effendi 79

Stories with the Greatest Holy Leaf Bahíyyih Khánum 97

Stories with the Holy Mother Munírih Khánum 107

Stories about Hand of the Cause of God Amatu'l-Bahá Rúhíyyih Khánum as a Child 109

History of the Children 113

Notes 123

Bibliography 131

Index 135

Acknowledgments

While I have heard—and shared—these stories all my life, it has taken the support of many people to bring them together in this little book. Everyone who has worked on this book has done so with great love for the Holy Family and the Bahá'í holy places in the Holy Land.

My gratitude goes first to my family. My mother Iran Furútan Muhájir has helped me at every step with every decision about the compilation and publication. Together we found an envelope of photographs that my father, the Hand of the Cause of God Raḥmatu'lláh Muhájir, had sent to her in 1977 that contained exactly the photographs we needed and that are now included in this book. My children Johnathan Abbas Mohadjer Cook and Amelia Rúḥíyyih Mohadjer Cook first heard these stories from us while on pilgrimage, and they inspired this collection. Johnathan has also read various drafts and made thoughtful suggestions. My mother-in-law Anne Lingelbach Cook's extensive library of Bahá'í books was a wonderful resource. My husband Robert Wallace Cook has joined me in presenting these stories to various audiences.

My thanks also go to Nat Yogachandra and Bahhaj Taherzadeh at the Bahá'í Publishing Trust of the United States for their immediate enthusiasm and encouragement when I first told them about the compilation, and to Christopher Martin for his meticulous editing.

I would also like to thank Edward Sevcik at the National Bahá'í Archives of the United States for the beautiful high-quality photographs he provided.

Publisher's Note

The reader may notice some inconsistency in spellings. For example, in some stories, the Most Great Prison is spelled Acre, while in others it is spelled 'Akká. Additionally, the reader may note that some accounts use the British spellings of words, while others use American spellings. These differences have resulted from the preservation, as much as possible, of the original wording of each author's account of these priceless remembrances.

This book contains multiple accounts of encounters and interactions with members of the Holy Family. Such accounts are to be considered the recollections of those who recorded them, as "pilgrims' notes," and not as authenticated renderings of the Holy Family's words and actions.

Introduction

This little book includes charming, tender, and humorous stories about the interactions of children with the Holy Family in the Bahá'í holy places in the Holy Land. Within its pages, you will find stories of how the Holy Family lovingly fostered the spiritual development of each child and youth, whether from the East or the West. These stories show spirituality, generosity, playfulness, hospitality, joy, instruction, education, kindness, and love.

We are fortunate that twenty-one of these children and youth shared their experiences and that several adults also wrote down their observations—these stories are reflected here in their own voices.

Professor Suheil Bushrú'í, who lived in the Holy Land as a child, once said about the Beloved Guardian Shoghi Effendi:

I was young, very young really, when I first came to be aware of that majestic figure of Shoghi Effendi. I am reminded of these two lines from the English poet Wordsworth:

Bliss it was in that dawn to be alive,
But to be young was very heaven.

Indeed it was.*

---

* Bushrú'í, "Memories of Shoghi Effendi," 2012.

My hope is that these stories will delight you, will draw you closer to the Holy Family, and will inspire you to strive to follow their example and make the lives of all children heavenly.

And if you have the privilege of going on pilgrimage to the holy places where these stories took place, perhaps you will take a moment to remember these children and how they were forever blessed by their time with the Holy Family.

Gisu Mohadjer Cook
Potomac, Maryland

Stories with the Blessed Beauty Bahá'u'lláh

The Greatest Holy Leaf told this story about the suffering of the innocent children on their first day in the prison in 'Akká, and the kindness of Bahá'u'lláh (1868)[1]:

> Then came another time of heart-sickening suffering. The mothers who had babes at breast had no milk for them, for lack of food and drink, so the babes could not be pacified or quieted. The larger children were screaming for food and water, and could not sleep or be soothed. The women were fainting.
>
> Under these conditions, my Brother ['Abdu'l-Bahá] spent the first part of the night passing about among the distressed people, trying to pacify them, and in appealing to the soldiers not to be so heartless as to allow women and children to suffer so. About midnight He succeeded in getting a message to the governor. We were then sent a little water and some cooked rice; but the latter was so full of grit and smelled so badly that only the strongest stomach could retain it. The water the children drank; but the rice only the strongest could eat. Later on, some of our people in unpacking their goods found some pieces of the bread which had been brought from Gallipoli, and a little sugar. With these a dish was prepared for the

1

Blessed Perfection, who was very ill. When it was taken to Him, He said: "I command you to take this to the children." So it was given to them, and they were somewhat quieted.

The next morning conditions were no better; there was neither water nor food that could be eaten. My Brother sent message after message to the governor, appealing in behalf of the women and children. At length he sent us water and some prisoners' bread; but the latter was worse even than the rice—appearing and tasting as though earth had been mixed with the flour. My Brother also succeeded in getting permission to send out a servant, guarded by four soldiers, to buy food.[2]

The Prison of ʻAkká

The story of Badíʻ's extraordinary courage (1869):

. . . Bahá'u'lláh revealed a long and detailed epistle for the Sháh of Persia. Those who have studied it realize that this epistle is a heavenly book containing scientific and spiritual teachings. Bahá'u'lláh purposed to send this Tablet by a messenger who would give it into the Sháh's own hands . . .

Now Badí' was a youth of seventeen, and at that time was in Acre and in the presence of Bahá'u'lláh. Before his arrival in Acre, His Holiness Bahá'u'lláh told His followers there that the messenger who was to carry this Tablet to the Sháh would ere long arrive.

One day, when some friends were gathered together His Holiness Bahá'u'lláh took the Tablet and holding it in his hand, said: "Who is the one who will carry this to the Sháh of Persia?"

Badí', like a flame of fire, sprang from his seat and bowing down before Bahá'u'lláh said: "I will carry this Tablet." Bahá'u'lláh asked the question a second time; and the youth repeated his supplication.

Bahá'u'lláh called the third time, and the third time Badí' petitioned that he might carry the Tablet.

So Bahá'u'lláh gave him the wonderful Tablet, and Badí' took it, and started on his great mission.[3]

Gifts for a beloved grandson (sometime between 1882–1887):

Bahá'u'lláh sent this Tablet to His grandson Ḥusayn Effendi, the son of 'Abdu'l-Bahá:

O Ḥusayn Effendi! Upon thee be God's peace and His favour. Yesterday We were in Junaynih. Some pomegranate was found and sent. We instructed Mustafa, should he find something else in the city, to procure it and send it with the pomegranate. A small sum was also sent.[4]

3

Zia Mabsoot Baghdádí's story of how he received a new name (between 1882–1892):

I had the greatest honor and privilege to see Bahá'u'lláh and sit at His feet many days and nights in this Mansion. Here He used to hold my hand while walking to and fro in His large room, revealing Tablets, chanting the prayers with the most charming and melodious voice, while one of the attendants took them down. Here I saw Him teaching and blessing the pilgrims who came from all lands. On hot days He would take me with Him to the outer alcove of the Mansion where it was somewhat cooler. I would stand in a corner with folded arms, my eyes fixed on His incomparable countenance, while the gentle breezes blew on His soft jet black hair which reached almost to the waist, flowing beneath the taj, like a crown, that covered His head and a part of His broad, full, high forehead.

From His light-colored garments which were similar to those of all the ancient prophets, I had always inhaled the fragrance of the pure attar of roses. At times He would spend half an hour on the alcove, and my eyes would remain fixed on His majestic face. But whenever He glanced at me with His brown, piercing, yet most affectionate eyes, then I had to turn mine away and look down at the floor.

At my birth, Bahá'u'lláh named me "Zia" (Light) and gave me the Turkish title "Effendi." But on my first visit to Him, when He inquired about my health, I replied in Arabic "Mabsoot" (I am happy). He questioned, "How is your father?" I answered "Mabsoot"; and "How is your mother?" He asked. "Mabsoot" was my reply. He laughed heartily and after that He always called me Mabsoot Effendi (The Happy One).[5]

Muḥammad-i-Tabrízí's story of receiving extra sweets from Bahá'u'lláh:

Áqá Muḥammad-i-Tabrízí has recounted how, as a child of four or five, he would go with his family to the Mansion of Bahjí each Friday, as was customary among the believers at that time, to attain the presence of the Blessed Beauty. They would stay all day, using the rooms on the lower floor of the Mansion.

During one of these visits the grown-ups were resting in their rooms at noontime; as it was a warm day, he left his room and wandered to the upper floor of the Mansion where he entered the large hall. Ambling about he eventually came to the room where food was stored, and here he noticed a bag filled with sugar. Instinctively he took a handful, put it in his mouth, then filled both hands before leaving the storeroom. Back in the hall, he froze in his tracks upon seeing the Blessed Beauty pacing to and fro there. Slowly and in a gentle manner, Bahá'u'lláh came towards him, cast a loving glance at his hands and then led the little boy towards a large table in the middle of the hall. Picking up a plate of candies, He offered one to the child who, with closed fist, accepted it. "It seems you like sweets," Bahá'u'lláh said. "Eat well! Goodbye. And may God protect you."

Years later, Áqá Muḥammad would explain to his fellow believers how no one at that time could appreciate his childish sentiments and the love he felt in his heart for the Blessed Beauty—a love which, from that moment, had never left him.[6]

'Azízu'lláh Varqá's story of meeting the Blessed Beauty (1891):

When the maternal grandfather, the father,[7] ['Azízu'lláh] and Rúḥu'lláh arrived in 'Akká they went to the room of the

The Mansion of Bahjí

secretary of Bahá'u'lláh. It was furnished with a mat and they sat down on this, for they had been told that Bahá'u'lláh would come to this room to meet them. In the distance there were steps leading to an upper room and the father told 'Azízu'lláh to go and stay near those steps to watch the approach of the Blessed Beauty and then to inform them. The child went but when he looked and saw Bahá'u'lláh at the head of the stairs he mounted several steps and knelt at the feet of His Lord. He was crying so hard his very bones were shaking. Bahá'u'lláh stopped and made him happy and they came down the stairway together, the little boy just behind Bahá'u'lláh. It was a great meeting, but when the visitation was over, the father said to his little son: "Why did you not do what I asked you to do! Why did you not run and tell us?" 'Azízu'lláh replied: "I do not know. I do not know how I mounted those steps, I was not conscious that I went up the stairs."[8]

'Azízu'lláh Varqá's story of being present while a Tablet was revealed (1891):

One day I was in Bahá'u'lláh's Presence with the whole family and He called for the secretary to bring ink and paper quickly and in the same moment He requested us all to go. I was just a child, but seeing this haste to send everyone away, I had a great longing to be present sometime when a Tablet is revealed. . . . A few weeks later in the Garden at Bahjí, when I was playing with some children, the door of the home was opened and [someone] called me and said that Bahá'u'lláh wished to see me. I ran to His room and entering I saw that He was chanting revealed Tablets and poems. So entering His room that day, I thought everything was the same as on other days. . . . I stood near the door which I had entered, and was only a few moments in the room when I began trembling in my whole body. I felt I could not stand any more on my feet. His Holiness Bahá'u'lláh turning to me said "Good-bye." As I lifted the curtain to go out, I fell on the threshold and was unconscious. . . . they poured rose water and cold water on my face until I revived. . . . Then I understood why Bahá'u'lláh in haste dismissed everybody. It is because the people cannot endure it, there is such a Power in the room.[9]

Rúḥu'lláh Varqá's story of teaching the Bahá'í Faith (1891):

Rúḥu'lláh, the son of Varqá[10] and himself a martyr, was but seven years old when, accompanied by his father and brother, 'Azízu'lláh, he had the honour of visiting the Ancient Beauty.

Jokingly, Bahá'u'lláh asked him what he would do if the promised Qá'im awaited by the Shí'ihs [the Báb] were suddenly to appear and come face to face with him.

Rúḥu'lláh unhesitatingly replied: "With the assistance of the Blessed Beauty, I would inform him of the teachings, and he would become a Bahá'í."[11]

Rúḥu'lláh Varqá's explanation of the Return of the Prophets (1891):

> One day Bahá'u'lláh asked Rúḥu'lláh "What did you do today?"
>
> He replied, "I was having lessons. . . ."
>
> Bahá'u'lláh asked, "What subject were you learning?"
>
> "Concerning the return [of the prophets]," said Rúḥu'lláh.
>
> "Will you explain what that means?" Bahá'u'lláh demanded.
>
> He replied: "By return is meant the return of realities and qualities."
>
> Bahá'u'lláh, questioning him further, said: "These are exactly the words of your teacher and you are repeating them like a parrot. Tell me in your own words your own understanding of the subject."
>
> "It is like cutting a flower from a plant this year," answered Rúḥu'lláh. "Next year's flower will look exactly like this one, but it is not the same."
>
> The Blessed Beauty praised the child for his intelligent answer and often called him Jináb-i-Muballigh (his honour, the Bahá'í teacher).[12]

Ṭarázu'lláh Samandarí's story of receiving a gift of new clothes for Naw-Rúz (1892):

> On the morning of Naw-Rúz, the Abhá Beauty sent me a gift, from the Mansion at Bahjí to the caravanserai where I was staying. It included a qabá [a long robe]—of silk, striped with cotton, and made in Syria—a shirt, undergarments, a sash of linen, and a pair of socks. You can imagine what joy and happiness possessed this feeble servant![13]

Ṭarázu'lláh Samandarí's story of celebrating Naw-Rúz (1892):

A number of pilgrims and friends resident in the Holy Land were permitted to attain His sanctified presence on Naw-Rúz in the Garden of Junaynih.

. . . They provided us with conveyances and brought us there [from Haifa]. . . . We came to Junaynih, where we found Bahá'u'lláh. So there, too, I entered His presence. About thirty of us, perhaps, were guests at luncheon: among the poets were, it seems to me, Jináb-i-'Andalíb, Ustád Muḥammad-'Alí was there, and Nabíl-i-A'ẓam. The last-named [Nabíl] and 'Andalíb sang verses that day, from an ode. Lunch had been made ready for us.

They had prepared a lamb for our luncheon; cooked it in the stove; and brought it in on a large tray, which they placed on the table in Bahá'u'lláh's room. I was at that moment standing near Him, with my arms folded across my chest. He touched the lamb with His finger and said, "Take it away."

They took it out to the other room where they had laid the luncheon cloth on the floor. We had bread too, with the lamb. We all ate luncheon there. Following the meal, it seems to me there was also a revelation of verses. I listened a little from outside the door; I heard a little. Then, that afternoon, Bahá'u'lláh was to return to the Mansion of Bahjí. There was a white donkey which, I know, Haji Ghulám-'Alí Káshání had brought to Bahá'u'lláh at that time. The Blessed Beauty mounted, and a servant held an umbrella over Him, for a light rain was falling. I also accompanied Him. On His right hand, the servant held up the umbrella, while I was on His left. And thus we came from Junaynih to the Mansion of Bahjí.[14]

Ṭarázu'lláh Samandarí's story of celebrating the First Day of Riḍván (1892):

> It was the first day of Riḍván. . . .
>
> To begin with He gave us candies, which they brought down from upstairs [in the Mansion of Bahjí] and passed around. We ate all the candies. . . . We were five people—the first group to come out and pay our respects on the Riḍván Festival. . . .
>
> When we arrived [upstairs], we knelt before Bahá'u'lláh and remained seated on the floor in that position. The Blessed Beauty was seated on a chair. His room was carpeted with a mat woven of marsh reeds; there was nothing else in the room. He addressed us lovingly. After His expressions of loving-kindness . . . He began to chant the Lawḥ-i-Sulṭán, the Tablet to the Sháh—some part of it.
>
> . . . That day I witnessed in Him two states of being: one was His overwhelming meekness, and no meekness greater than His can be conceived—a condition of evanescence and meekness referred to by Him in many Tablets. The other was the condition of might, of the power and authority of the Supreme Pen. . . .
>
> Then He brought the reading to a close and said, with that heavenly music of His voice: "Ṭaráz Effendi, stand up!" I stood up.
>
> They had brought a quantity of roses from Junaynih, red roses, fresh from the bush, perhaps thirty or forty in all, and placed them on a mat or cushion in His room, on a white cloth.
>
> He said, "Give a rose to each one present here." I took them up, and I gave one rose to each. Then I stood waiting.

He said, "And what about My share?" I took one and offered it to Him.

Then He said, "Take one yourself, as well." I took one myself.

And He dismissed us, saying, "Go in God's care— Fí amán'u'lláh."[15]

The Garden of Riḍván

Ṭarázu'lláh Samandarí's story about celebrating Riḍván (1892):

During the Festival of Riḍván, the Blessed Beauty decided to visit the Garden of Riḍván near 'Akká. By this, a further blessing was brought to that exalted Paradise, a place mentioned in the holy books of the past. All of the friends and believers in the vicinity, and all the pilgrims, with faces of joy, rushed to that everlasting Paradise—the envy of all the gardens on earth. This feeble servant also had the honor of sharing in that meeting.

'Andalíb . . . had composed an ode, and he read it in the presence of the Blessed Beauty, who was standing on the veranda of His room in the garden. All the friends, disciples, pilgrims, and guests fixed their eyes on the face of the Beloved. We were standing in rows. He showered unlimited bounties upon all of us. With His own hands, He gave rose water, sweetmeats, and an orange to each one.

'Andalíb received the distinction of being given a bottle of rose water and two oranges!—a special prize for his poetry, for the ode he had read.[16]

Ṭarázu'lláh Samandarí's story about receiving a gift of dates from Bahá'u'lláh, and the gentle lesson on contentment (1892):

Once—it was sunset—I had the honor of being in His presence. Javád-i-Qazvíní was there, and he was asking certain questions and receiving answers. Bahá'u'lláh extended to us His utmost care and grace. He always called me Ṭaráz Effendi.

There was a tin of dates from Baṣra. The Blessed Beauty took one. He gave the seed to Javád, saying: "Look how small the seed is." Then He gave me a handful of dates. When He reached for the tin a second time, I quickly lifted the hem of my robe to take more. But He said: "If you take too much, it will cause you harm. This place is the Most Great Prison!" He then gave the dates to Javád.

We then had the honor of hearing His words: "Fí amán'u'lláh—go in God's care," and we left the Holy Presence overwhelmed with joy.[17]

Ṭarázu'lláh Samandarí's story about paying respect to the departed (1892):

On another occasion, one of the believers, a woman greatly blessed and favored by the Blessed Beauty, passed away. It was heard that at the hour of dawn prayer, He had gone to her bedside. Then He directed that all should attend her burial, and all should first come into His presence. Here each of us was anointed with rose water by His hand. I was the last to be anointed by Him that day; I received the 'aṭṭár from His holy hand, and touched His hand. . . .

It was at Bahjí in the great court. He stood in front of a curtain. It was there that I received the rose water. Then He commanded us, "Go, all of you, to the burial."[18]

Ṭarázu'lláh Samandarí's story of running to protect the gift that he had received (1892):

Three times, on three different days, in the afternoons, I had the opportunity to enter the presence of Bahá'u'lláh in His blessed tent which was erected on the northern side of the Mansion of Bahjí. The field was covered with red wildflowers and the tent was pitched amidst them. Three memorable meetings were held in this place. . . . On [the third] day, a meal was served, halim—a porridge, a health food. . . .

The Most Pure Being, Bahá'u'lláh, was seated in a corner of the tent. There were not enough chairs. Some people sat in them at Bahá'u'lláh's bidding. Those left standing, He asked to sit. "Be seated, be seated," He insisted. They sat on the ground. . . .[19]

When He said to sit down, I realized that if I did, because I was small (I was seventeen then) perhaps I would not be able to see Him clearly. It occurred to me that I should go to a certain corner of the tent, the part called the closet. So I quietly slipped out of the tent, went around to the back, and got into the closet. There I was not more than a meter away from Bahá'u'lláh. From that vantage I could see Him clearly, and should He speak, I could hear Him as well.

I was there when [a person] chanted Muṣíbát-i-'Álíyát. When he had finished, a tray of baklava and a tray of oranges which had stood prepared was passed around. First the Blessed Beauty took one, then the others were distributed. But no one knew about me being in the back of the tent; and since nobody knew it, I did not get an orange.

After the meeting was over, Bahá'u'lláh arose. I hastily came out of my corner and entered the tent, standing there, arms folded across my chest. As He issued forth, I bowed low before Him and He gave me the orange which He still held in His hand. He proceeded then to the Mansion.

But the youth had discovered the fact that Bahá'u'lláh had given me His own orange! And they came after me to wrest it away. So I ran and ran, dodging here and there outside the Mansion, devouring the orange as I went.[20]

Ṭarázu'lláh Samandarí's story of a day with 'Abdu'l-Bahá, and a lesson on the station of the Master (1892):

. . . on a certain day the Master took me, around noon, to the mosque in 'Akká. There He asked me, "Do you know the prayer?" I answered, "No, may I be Thy sacrifice." He then told me, "Sit in the mosque, and we will enter soon. Then whatever I do, do the same."

I stayed with Him all that day. When the prayer was over, we went out of the mosque; and as we approached the gate of 'Akká, the Master said, "I wish to go with you into the

The Shrine of Bahá'u'lláh, the Mansion of Bahjí, and the extensive gardens

blessed presence of Bahá'u'lláh at Bahjí. Have you an umbrella?" I said yes. And as it was sprinkling a little, He told me: "Go, fetch your umbrella, I will be walking outside the gate until you come." In those days, I was very fleet of foot. I ran like the wind to the caravanserai—it was a good distance, too—got my umbrella and took it back to 'Abdu'l-Bahá outside the gate.

Alone with Him, I went to Bahjí. The moment that the Mansion of Bahjí came into view, 'Abdu'l-Bahá got down on His knees and bowed His forehead to the ground. Then He rose, and together we entered the Mansion. . . . Whenever 'Abdu'l-Bahá approached the Mansion, Bahá'u'lláh would be watching for His arrival from His latticed window. As soon as He saw 'Abdu'l-Bahá coming, He would say, "His Excellency, Áqá, is coming. Go out and welcome Him." This matter was always current and known, and Bahá'u'lláh would make people mindful of it. Whenever He presented 'Abdu'l-Bahá to anyone—to women, men, to young or old, He would always refer to Him as "Sarkár Áqá—His Excellency, the Master." And when they were alone, He would naturally say "Áqá."[21]

Ṭarázu'lláh Samandarí's story about speaking with Bahá'u'lláh for the first time, and the gentle lesson on the Covenant (1892):

> . . . I went alone from 'Akká to Bahjí. When I reached the foot of the Mansion steps—there are twenty-two steps—I saw a young child there and I asked that child: "Where is His Holiness Bahá'u'lláh?"
>
> "He is in His own room," came the answer.
>
> "And what," I asked, "is He engaged in?"
>
> "He is pacing the floor," the child said.
>
> "Who is in His presence?" I asked again.
>
> "No one."
>
> "Not even a servant?" I said.
>
> "No."
>
> I said, "Go. Say to Him, it is Ṭaráz. He has not been in Your presence for several days. May he approach You now?"
>
> The child left, speedily returned, and told me: "He says: 'Bismi'lláh—come in the name of God.'" When I heard the word *Bismi'lláh,* my limbs began to shake. I don't know how I climbed up those twenty-two steps to His room. He was still pacing the floor. I bowed low, then stood with my arms folded across my chest. He came over to me, and He drew His hand across my face and head, expressing infinite grace and favor.
>
> Then He asked how I was, and after that He said, "In 'Akká, do you not seek out the presence of Sarkár Áqá, the Master?"

Until that day, I had never unsealed my lips in His holy presence. Now I answered: "I attend upon Him day and night, may I be Thy sacrifice."

He smiled. "Then why do you complain," He said, "that you have not been in My presence? Why do you complain that you have not been in My presence? For your own comfort and well-being, We had you stay in 'Akká, but this is your home. You have permission to come here at any hour, at any time, morning, noon, or night."

I was blessed by Him repeatedly that day, and truly it was He who sowed the love of the Covenant in my inmost heart, and wrote it there with the words of His holy mouth.[22]

'Abdu'l-Bahá with Bahíyyih Winckler

Stories with the Beloved Master 'Abdu'l-Bahá

Remembering His son Ḥusayn Effendi (1885–1886):

> [O]ne day the Master said: "I had a little son. When he was three or four, and I would be asleep, he would come and very gently, very softly, slip into bed beside me. It was an indescribable joy." A year or so later the little boy was gone.[1]

The importance of good conduct (1901):

> Despite the enormous press of work, the Master found time once in every week to hold a class for small Bahá'í children. Here they would recite the short Tablets they had learned by heart and bring samples of their handwriting to show Him. He loved them. He showed great concern, wishing them to learn the principles of Bahá'í conduct. Although He was firm, He strictly forbade anyone to strike a child or use the customary rod or harshly punish them. He told their parents and teachers to emphasize the importance of good conduct and said that in this way, if the child failed in some particular, the very reminding the child that he had failed would impress that child as a severe punishment. The child would thus learn to avoid even

the slightest failure in good conduct and grow up to recognize good conduct as the true mark of a Bahá'í.[2]

William Dodge's and Wendell Dodge's story of their arrival (1901):

At 4:15 in the afternoon of November 16th, 1901, 'Abdu'l-Bahá entered our room and greeted us. We had just arrived at His Holy household in the prison city of 'Akká, Syria having traveled in a carriage driven by two horses along the shore of the Mediterranean from Haifa. 'Abdu'l-Bahá said: "Welcome, my boys," and chanted a prayer for my brother Wendell and me. Wendell was 18 and I was 21. . . .[3]

'Abdu'l-Bahá sitting in His carriage along the beach on His way back to Haifa from Bahjí, October 1921

William Dodge's and Wendell Dodge's story of their meals and lessons (1901):

We stayed with 'Abdu'l-Baha in His household 19 days: November 16th, 1901 to December 4th, 1901. Every day breakfast was served to us in our room. The noon day meal and the evening dinner we had with 'Abdu'l-Bahá at His table. Generally about 16 Persian believers attended each meal, making 19 present. . . . Each morning after breakfast 'Abdu'l-Bahá came to our room and greeted us. He was gracious, considerate and always concerned with our comfort. At every meal 'Abdu'l-Bahá gave us lessons and allowed us plenty of time to record His remarks in our notebooks.[4]

William Dodge's and Wendell Dodge's story of being happy (1901):

Although 'Abdu'l-Bahá was a serious expounder of the Bahá'í Faith He had a fine sense of humor. One day at dinner, we were eating soup, a nice thick soup. Leaving my spoon in the plate I raised my hand to adjust my collar. As I brought down my hand my elbow came in contact with the handle of the spoon. And soup was spread upon the whiskers of the Persian believer on my right. Of course, I was terribly embarrassed. However, 'Abdu'l-Bahá, observing the incident quickly said: "Do not worry. That is a blessing" and laughed aloud. My brother Wendell then remarked: "Who gets the blessing, Bill, you or the friend with the whiskers?" And 'Abdu'l-Bahá laughed again.

Wendell and I were so glad to be with 'Abdu'l-Bahá. At some times we were quite jolly. We were mere boys of 18 and 21. Our interpreter . . . told us that we must be reverent, that when we entered the presence of the Master we must bow our heads, clasp our hands, avoid smiling. Of course we felt the rebuke.

So the next time we entered the dining room, our heads were bowed, our hands clasped, and we did not smile. 'Abdu'l-Bahá passed quickly by us. He seemed to ignore us. We felt further re-buked. Returning to our room we wondered why 'Abdu'l-Bahá seemed different in His attitude toward us. Well, we decided that we were not good actors. So when we entered the dining room for the next meal, we smiled. 'Abdu'l-Bahá smiled. He came over to us, took us in his arms and said: "That's the way I want you boys to act—be natural, be happy."[5]

William Dodge's and Wendell Dodge's story of receiving gifts (1901):

During the early days of the Bahá'í Faith in the United States many of the believers wore a ring containing a stone on which was engraved the greatest name. 'Abdu'l-Bahá came to our room on November 24th, 1901 with ten of those stones. He kissed each one and then handed five of them to Wendell and five to me and then chanted a prayer for us.[6]

William Dodge's and Wendell Dodge's story of how the Master remembered their parents (1901):

'Abdu'l-Bahá often talked to us about mother and father. They had visited Him in 1900. . . . 'Abdu'l-Bahá told us that He dreamed that our father was with Him again. He said that although Mr. Dodge was not with Him in person he was al-ways with Him spiritually.[7]

Badí' Bushrú'í's story of meeting 'Abdu'l-Bahá (1902):

As I climbed the stairs of the house of the Master and reached the Master's room, I was swooned by the life-sustaining melodies of "welcome, welcome." As my eyes beheld His elegant countenance, I lost all consciousness. . . . 'Abdu'l-Bahá had a kind and merciful regard for this feeble one, and the hospitality of the Greatest Holy Leaf, opened the doors of happiness and joy from every side.[8]

Badí' Bushrú'í's story of learning to read and write from a renowned Persian Bahá'í calligrapher (1902):

'Abdu'l-Bahá ordered me to write my homework in Persian under the supervision of Mishkín-Qalam and to learn reading in Persian and English.[9]

The Master's attention to education, as told by Dr. Youness Khán (1903):

One day, when I was totally absorbed in my translation work, suddenly feeling a presence I raised my head and beheld the blessed figure of the Master standing in front of my desk. I stood up and bowed.

"Jináb-i-Khán, I have a favour to ask you and you have no choice but to accept," said 'Abdu'l-Bahá.

Of course, my response to such kind and loving words was more bows, broad joyful smiles, and expressions of gratitude and delight.

"One hour each day, you must teach English to the children of the friends. Áqá Mírzá Núri'd-Dín will teach them Persian and you must teach them English," He thus instructed.

From the following day, a room in the pilgrim house was allocated for this purpose. The room was prepared, benches and desks were brought in and I began the service with which I had been honoured by the Master.

There were some twenty students divided into two groups. Lessons began and before long rapid progress was achieved. The children enjoyed quite a few benefits in their training, appropriate to the prevailing conditions of austerity and hardship in the Most Great Prison. In addition to the study of Persian, English, mathematics and other lessons, they had to master a trade or vocation. Despite a rampant scarcity of all goods, each child had to have a desk.

Training in shoe-making, carpentry, and tailoring were more readily available to the children and therefore most of them were already engaged as apprentices in these trades.

The Master paid a great deal of attention to all facets of education of the young. Each and every one of them, regardless of age or any other consideration, was educated under His direct and close supervision. . . .

The late Mishkín-Qalam taught penmanship. Even the great Zaynu'l-Muqarrabín had been assigned to teach Arabic and Bahá'í Writings. The sun of generosity shone on all, the showers of confirmation fell upon everyone. . . .

While I was engaged in teaching English, I noted that 'Abdu'l-Bahá's desire for the education of the children was so intense that despite the overwhelming pressures of His all-important work, to our amazement He found time to attend to the most minute details of their work.

In addition to His personal visits every few weeks, which included His enquiring into each pupil's progress in school and reviewing the results of their quarterly exams, He spoke to them at length every Friday about the significance of their education and training. . . . This method of education continued until my departure from 'Akká. For some time after that, Mírzá Núri'd-Dín continued my classes, and thus the children of the Emigrants, who served the threshold of the Centre of the Covenant in that Most Great Prison where they faced great difficulty in even earning a meagre livelihood, were not deprived of the benefits of education.[10]

The Master's interest in each child's progress as observed by Dr. Youness Khán:

> . . . now is the time for the celebration of the Baháʾí children. But ʿAbduʾl-Bahá has not as yet found an opportunity to rest.
>
> The schoolchildren are standing in line according to their height, holding their completed handwriting exercises and waiting for ʿAbduʾl-Baháʾs arrival so that they too may receive His heart-warming attention, His generous favours and gifts, and His spiritual teachings. First, ʿAbduʾl-Bahá walks quickly to the nearby sink to wash away the effects of the many blemishes and marks left on His hands by . . . the poor, eager to extract their share from His hands. Then He prepares to meet the children.
>
> Here, some twenty-two or three children are standing in line. After bestowing upon them words of affection and love, He first enquires from their teacher after their manner of conduct and behaviour. Then, He takes the completed exercise sheet from an older child and reviews it. The reed pen, already cut to a suitable tip, is ready in the hand of the student, who gives it to the Master.
>
> "This must be written this way. This letter should be written somewhat higher. The straight lines have not been adhered to." In short, He reviews each one, praising some and giving proper instruction to others. "This time you have written better," or "Your handwriting has got worse!" When He reaches

the younger children He treats them with special affection and shares with them a few humorous words. Then at random He takes their English homework and asks some of the students a few questions. He paces up and down the line, paying attention to the details of their lessons. He even examines the cleanliness of their hands. Finally, he offers some advice regarding certain general topics such as one's manners and conduct, then He talks about turning to God and about the nature of religion.

Gradually His words gain momentum, and the pilgrims and residents who are standing some distance away move closer. As He paces up and down, 'Abdu'l-Bahá's words become so moving that one feels transformed, finding oneself in a different world. The effect is so intense that while soaring in the world of spirit one becomes aware of one's past and future shortcomings. Each according to his capacity and understanding clearly discerns that reality which is sanctified beyond any word or mention. On the one hand he forgets the world of being and all that is therein, and on the other he beholds the invisible and recognizes the unrecognizable. On the wings of spirit he soars to such heights that he would refuse the possession of this world were it to be offered to him.

God be praised, for the sake of these children the bounty of utterance has surged to such lofty heights, carrying His listeners to heavenly worlds beyond. It is to be hoped that through this bounty, worldly listeners may receive spiritual perfections and His earth-bound devotees may discover heavenly virtues.

As soon as the talk ends, out comes the moneybag. There are plenty of quarter-majídí and two-qurushi pieces to go around. He starts with the top student and works down to the smaller children. What makes it more wonderful is that as He passes out the coins He continues to entertain the children with humorous remarks and funny stories. Having completed the task, He takes a seat in the bírúní reception room, and along with the rest of the friends enjoys a round of sweet coffee.[11]

'Abdu'l-Bahá writing

A story about special celebrations:

> . . . Áqá Riḍá' Qannád, who had been with his Master
> throughout the terrible early days . . . took us to see the Khán.
> This was an inn, where the pilgrims used to stay in that time,
> when, at length, rules being a little relaxed, and the believers
> having discovered where their Beloved One was imprisoned,
> made long, arduous journeys, hoping to see Him. Here we
> came to the long, stone-floored room, where the friends used
> to spread out their bedding and rest, also the rows of little
> rooms where families encamped. . . . The Khán is a wonder-
> fully picturesque building, built round a large courtyard, with
> rows of rounded arches and columns on three sides.
>
> Here the Master's custom was to assemble all the poor, es-
> pecially the children, of 'Akká, on Feast Days, both Christian
> and Muslim, also on the anniversary of the Sulṭán's corona-
> tion. Here he regaled them with sweets, cakes, fruit, and tea.
> He had the middle fountain filled with Sharbat, which was a
> great treat.[12]

The Master with the little children of the household as observed by
Mary Lucas (1905):

> Every morning [at seven o'clock] it is the custom of the
> household to meet in the large sitting room, where tea is
> served, and the little children of the family come and chant for
> the Master while he drinks his tea. . . .
>
> It is beautiful to see the Master with the little children and
> observe His consideration for their childish troubles. One
> morning [a girl of] about two years old, was talking to the

Master in the most serious way, telling Him with expressive gesticulations her difficulty. Something had gone crosswise with her. The Master without a smile listened most attentively. This was a great lesson. When we consider what the Master has to bear—a man of ordinary strength could not endure it one hour—yet when a little child comes and confides in Him her trouble, how tender, how loving He is! How forgetful of self!

Shall I ever forget the heavenly smile and love expressed in that beautiful Face when this tiny maiden was chanting for Him a Tablet! Every now and then she would forget a word, and He would gently chant it for her, while He drank His tea, seated in the corner of the divan. How the little children love Him![13]

Arna True's story of arriving in 'Akká (1907):

Soon after [Corinne] and Arna had settled into the room, [someone] came to the door bearing a gift of three roses from ['Abdu'l-Bahá] for them and their fellow-pilgrim. . . .

A few moments later, they heard the Master's steps in the hall and 'Abdu'l-Bahá appeared with a handful of hyacinths, pink and purple, which He divided into three parts. They were the first hyacinths of the season, gathered early that morning by the gardener. Such an outpouring of love, they felt, as He greeted them.

He spoke briefly, welcoming them to His home, and stating how happy he was that people from the East and West were uniting. Through the power of the Word of God, He added, hatred between orientals and occidentals was diminishing and, eventually, that Word would be the cause of uniting their hearts.

Soon after He left, they were joined by [others] bringing Corinne and Arna each a tangerine, and also a gift from the Master.

When Corinne and Arna entered the small dining-room for midday dinner, the Master took them by the hand and led them to the table. He seated Arna to His right, as His guest of honor.

. . . Late that afternoon the Master came to see them in their room, as He could not have tea (the evening meal) with them . . .[14]

Arna True's story of playing with the children and the Master (1907):

The first three days Arna seemed restless, even bored . . . At lunch one day, He turned to her and asked if she was happy. When she responded, "Yes, but not very," . . . 'Abdu'l-Bahá smiled, obviously pleased with Arna's candor, and asked if she would like to be with the Persian children in the other part of the house.

The Master's solution worked well. It didn't matter that the children couldn't understand English, and Arna didn't know Persian or Arabic. Her natural love for them was a language the youngsters understood. She taught the boys and girls, including 10-year-old Shoghi Effendi who had come for the weekend from his school in Haifa, all the American games she knew. One afternoon the Master entered the courtyard and stopped to watch Arna with an excited group of Persian children playing jump-rope. Impressed, He took a turn, turning the rope.[15]

Howard Kinney's story of eating macaroni (1909):

One day at lunch a huge dish of macaroni was put on the table. The Master, laughing, rose from His seat, took the platter in His own hands, brought it to little Howie's highchair and served him a very big helping. Then He told us that [he] had come to His door that morning, had taken off his shoes and left them at the door step, then had run to Him, the Master, where He was sitting by the window, thrown his arms around the Master's neck and whispered in His ear: "My Lord, can't we have macaroni for lunch?"

"He is never allowed it at home," laughed [his mother] Carrie.[16]

Howard Kinney's and Sandy Kinney's story of drinking tea (1909):

Tea was brought in—in the little clear glasses always used in 'Akká—and He served us with His own hands. Then, seating Himself again on the divan, He called the four children who were with us . . . Shoghi Effendi and [one other], and the two Kinney boys, and with a lavish tenderness, a super abundance of overflowing love, such as could only have come from the very Center and Source of Love, He drew all four to His knees, clasped them in His arms, which enclosed them all, gathered and pressed and crushed them to His Heart of hearts. Then He set them down on the floor and, rising, Himself brought their tea to them.

Words absolutely fail me when I try to express the divine picture I saw then. With the Christ-love radiating from Him with the intensest sweetness I have yet witnessed, He stooped to the floor Himself to serve the little children, the children of the East and the children of the West. He sat on the floor in their midst, He put sugar into their tea, stirred it and fed it to them, all the while smiling celestially, an infinite tenderness playing on the great Immortal Face like white light. I cannot express it![17]

Howard Kinney's and Sandy Kinney's story of visiting the Shrine of the Báb (1909):

> We left the Holy Tomb.
> "Come and I will show you My garden," said our Lord. "Come, follow Me."
> With the little children—Sandy pressed close to one side, Howard to the other—He led us. In folds indescribably graceful, His white robes blew about His Figure.[18]

A shawl for a little girl (1914):

> In the afternoon, some of the people took their children to see 'Abdu'l-Bahá. He received them with utmost kindness and generosity and even took off his own embroidered Persian shawl and with His blessed hands put it on the head of a little girl.[19]

Praise for the good conduct of the Bahá'í students:

> The students of Beirut [Syrian Protestant] College, some of whom were graduates of the medical college and some from the high school, arrived in Haifa to spend their vacation. The next morning they went to the garden and met 'Abdu'l-Bahá. With joy and praise he said to them: "The Bahá'í students in Beirut have so conducted themselves, both within and without

the college, that even the Protestants and members of the faculty have testified to their superiority. He who is possessed of good behavior is always happy, always at ease and every soul becomes attracted to him. There is nothing better than good conduct. . . ."[20]

'Abdu'l-Bahá walking outside His home, known as the House of the Master, at Number 7 Haparsim Street in Haifa

Badí' Bushrú'í's story of an evening with the Master (1914):

You enter a house full of different kinds of flowers—nature is indeed full of joy; birds are singing and humming bees, flying from one flower to another, prepare to go to their hives for rest. Twilight advances and all things are at peace. . . .

Suddenly, a voice is heard. A general hush comes over the pilgrims and the Master enters. He welcomes all and bids them take their seats. He begins to talk and all are eyes and ears. His words strike the right note in each man's life and this you can easily see from the expression of their faces. After an hour or so they are dismissed and the meeting is adjourned. The pilgrims start for the pilgrim's house on the top of Mount Carmel.[21]

Rúḥá Aṣdaq's story of the arrival of ʿAbduʾl-Bahá to the Holy Land (1913):

> It was a beautiful night with a gentle breeze caressing the sea and the brilliant stars above heralding a bright and clear day. Early at dawn, a ship could be seen in the distance, gracefully aiming its way along the bay. The Greatest Holy Leaf cast a deep look and said, "O vessel, what is it you bring that makes you sway so gracefully?" My heart began to beat fast as I heard these words, but I did not allow myself to think about them. A few hours went by and the ship approached Haifa harbor—its whistle could be heard far and wide. Only then were we aware of the arrival of the Centre of the Covenant [from His visits to the West].
>
> The main hall of the Master's house was being prepared for His arrival. All the pilgrims and members of the household gathered there. At the joyful time, ʿAbduʾl-Bahá descended from the carriage and made His way towards the house. The Greatest Holy Leaf . . . rushed towards Him and embraced Him. The beloved Master was so weak that after taking a few steps he began perspiring profusely and His clothes turned heavily moist such that the Greatest Holy Leaf placed an aba (cloak/robe) on His shoulders and together they made the way to His room. My younger sister Ṭáliʿa, upon witnessing the Master, began to faint. One American pilgrim took her hand in her arms and in a special accent said, "Say O Bahá! Say O Bahá!" We all wept and our breathing was heavy and difficult.
>
> After a brief rest and change of clothing, the beloved Master emerged from his room, sat before us and addressed those present with these words, "Welcome! Welcome!" He then uttered a few words which I was unable to understand. All I heard was a

heavenly melody which made its way to my heart and reverberated in my ear. After a prayer . . . He said, "May ye all remain in God's care." Then the ladies, with hearts overflowing with happiness, withdrew and permitted the equally anxious and tearful men to enter the hall. . . . And so it was on this auspicious day, 5 December 1913, events occurred that none would ever forget: all was engraved in our hearts and minds.[22]

Rúḥá Aṣdaq's story of a visit from 'Abdu'l-Bahá (1913–14):

. . . someone was beating at the door. I opened the door and Bashir, the servant of the Master, breathing heavily said, "Open the door, the Master is on His way." I was stunned. He shouted again, "The Master is coming." . . . At this moment 'Abdu'l-Bahá entered the house with his 'abá covering His head wet from the torrential rain and sat down in the reception room. After resting briefly He said, "I have come for your sake."

. . . I do not remember very well all that was said by the Master. I could never stare into the face of the Master and even if I tried I could not fathom the grandeur and majesty of His face. I was like a light bird freed from its surroundings and making its flight to the heavens. The tone of His voice had a heavenly sound and the reassuring and encouraging words stirred my entire being. I thought, "Lord, what bounty is it that has been granted to us? What have I done and how have I come to deserve such an honour to be alive this day and to have been brought up by such a father and mother? How am I to repay this bounty?" All I knew was that this hour and special bounty would never leave my thoughts. . . .

After consuming a cup of tea, slowly and gently the Beloved Master left us. None of us had the strength to utter a word. In our hearts we had nothing but eternal gratitude and thanks and this He could read from the depths of our inner being.[23]

Rúḥá Aṣdaq's story of breakfast (1913–14):

We were instructed to eat in the Master's house. Early in the morning, we woke up full of excitement to prepare ourselves for breakfast. There the samovar would be boiling and the breakfast table laid out. Aside from the members of the household, our mother and we three sisters were also present. The Beloved Master arrived, asked how we were and seated Himself. Everyone else seated themselves in their appointed places. . . . At this moment my heart began to pound uncontrollably, wondering whether 'Abdu'l-Bahá would ask me to chant—I, who had no voice at all! At this instant, with His eyes closed 'Abdu'l-Bahá directed Himself to Ṭáli'a and said, "Daughter of the martyr, chant." She chanted a prayer which referred to the believers of the East and West, North and South. After completing this prayer, the Beloved Master turned to the Greatest Holy Leaf and with a heart-warming smile said, "Khánum, see how appropriate was the prayer that she chanted." On another occasion He corrected her mistake after she had chanted an Arabic prayer. These morning meetings at the breakfast table I could never forget: the heated samovar from which the Greatest Holy Leaf would, with her own hands, offer tea to everyone and the Beloved Master enjoying the cheese, bread and olives which He so liked.[24]

Rúḥá Aṣdaq's story of the orange grove (1913–14):

Next to the kitchen there was a piece of land which had been cultivated by Ismá'íl Áqá as an orange grove during

'Abdu'l-Bahá's visit to Europe and North America. Before the return of 'Abdu'l-Bahá to the Holy Land no one dared venture near the small orange grove of Ismá'íl Áqá for fear of succumbing to the temptation of picking a tangerine. One day the Beloved Master went to the grove and picked some oranges and tangerines and with a radiant smile began eating them. Ismá'íl Áqá stood quietly behind the Master weeping with joy. After the Master left the grove having said words of encouragement, Ismá'íl Áqá cried out, "Now come and pick all you can eat. I have received approbation and my heart's wish. Come into the grove."[25]

'Abdu'l-Bahá in the Orange Grove at the House of the Master.

Rúḥá Aṣdaq's story of sitting away from the table (1913–14):

> Such was our state in the presence of 'Abdu'l-Bahá that we would lose all appetite. One day we requested the Greatest Holy Leaf that we be seated some distance away from the main table to eat and she approved. The next day when 'Abdu'l-Bahá arrived at the table the Greatest Holy Leaf said, "Master, they requested to be seated some distance away from the table." He replied, "Very well, it seems they don't eat anyway, all they do is smell the food." One day a local meal was prepared and the Beloved Master turned to us saying, "Don't eat this. It is a heavy meal and you are not used to it." The Beloved Master was satisfied with little food. Usually at the Master's house (the guest house) it was normal to cook ábgúsht (Persian stew). The Greatest Holy Leaf was always most attentive and careful and took special care of everyone. Many nights, without any of us being aware, she would take [my nephew] little Rúḥu'lláh aside and give him a lighter meal.[26]

Rúḥá Aṣdaq's story of her little nephew (1913–14):

> One day Rúḥu'lláh rushed to his mother without being aware of the presence of 'Abdu'l-Bahá. His mother with a gesture of her head signaled that he should return later. Rúḥu'lláh quickly grasped the situation and was about to retreat when 'Abdu'l-Bahá called him and said, "Come and sit here." He went and sat at the feet of 'Abdu'l-Bahá who ordered some tea and sweets for him, placed him on His knee, kissed him on the forehead and called him a "well-mannered man."[27]

Rúḥá Aṣdaq's story of singing Bahá'í odes and poems (1913–14):

> It was customary to carry out the chores while humming Bahá'í odes and poems. On occasion we would be permitted to leave and would go, either by carriage or by train, to Bahjí. When we would get off the train and started the journey on foot we would sing. Approaching the Mansion . . . we would sing a poem dedicated to 'Abdu'l-Bahá, raising our voices to resounding heights so that all could hear.[28]

Four little children come to the Master (1917):

> A Turkish official living in Haifa lost his position when the British occupation took place. He became very poor; he, with his wife and children, were in great want. They came to ask the help of Abbas Effendi, Who did much to soften their hardship. At length the poor man became ill; the Master sent a doctor to him, medicine, and many comforts.
>
> When about to die he asked for Abbas Effendi, and called his children. "Here," he said, "is your father, who will take care of you when I am gone."
>
> One morning four little children came to the house of Abbas Effendi; they said: "We want our father." The Master heard their voices and recognized them.
>
> "Oh! we have come to you, our other father is dead, and now you will take care of us, and be our father."
>
> The Master brought them in and gave them tea and cakes and sweets. He then went with the little ones to their home.

The father was not really dead, but had merely fainted; the children thought that he had passed away. However the next day he died.

The Master charged Himself with the whole responsibility of the doctor, nurse, and funeral. Then He provided the sad family with food, clothing, their travelling tickets, and other expenses to Turkey.[29]

A mother's story of a new garden for her child:

[A mother] related that when her child was ill, the Master came and gave two pink roses to the little one, then, turning to the mother, He said in His musical voice so full of love: "Be patient."

That evening the child passed away.

". . . there is a Garden of God. Human beings are trees growing therein. The Gardener is Our Father. When He sees a little tree in a place too small for her development, He prepares a suitable and more beautiful place, where she may grow and bear fruit. Then He transplants that little tree. The other trees marvel, saying: 'This is a lovely little tree. For what reason does the Gardener uproot it?'

"The Divine Gardener, alone, knows the reason.

"You are weeping, . . . but if you could see the beauty of the place where she is, you would no longer be sad. Your child is now free, and, like a bird, is chanting divine joyous melodies. If you could see that sacred Garden, you would not be content to remain here on earth. Yet this is where your duty now lies."[30]

Two little boys learn a fun new greeting:

> [Once] two little boys were in the Master's presence and bowed low, in the Persian fashion, the Master said: "No. Like this"—and, His back straight, He saluted.[31]

'Alí Yazdí's story of evenings at the House of the Master (1917):

> For over two months I lived on God's holy mountain.
>
> Every evening before sunset I had the bounty of being with 'Abdu'l-Bahá. I would join other believers gathered in front of the Master's house. The entrance had an iron gate, and inside the gate there was a garden. We would sit on the wall or parapet on each side of the wide gravel walk that led from the garden gate to the steps and wait for Him. He would come out with a cheerful and warm greeting, welcome all, and take His seat on the platform at the head of the wide stairs. The sun would be going down, and I remember it being very quiet in Haifa.
>
> Sometimes He sat relaxed and did not speak at all. But usually He spoke in His commanding voice, looking straight ahead as if speaking to posterity. He talked on Bahá'u'lláh, on Bahá'u'lláh's teachings, and on significant events in the history of the Faith. He told stories sprinkled with humor. And often He spoke of the believers around the world and of their progress in spreading the Faith. . . .
>
> Now and then He addressed individuals in the audience, asking them about their families, their work, their problems. Then He offered advice and help. Toward the end He asked one of the believers to chant verses from the Mathnaví of

Bahá'u'lláh. When the chanting ended, the meeting was over. 'Abdu'l-Bahá arose and entered the house. Dusk descended over Haifa.[32]

'Abdu'l-Bahá on the steps of the House of the Master

'Alí Yazdí's story of visiting the Shrine of the Báb (1917):

There were frequent trips to the Holy Shrine of the Báb. 'Abdu'l-Bahá rode an old horse-drawn, bus-like vehicle up the mountain. The rest of us walked the rocky road, past the Persian Pilgrim House to the terrace overlooking the city of Haifa and the blue bay beyond. In the distance lay the hazy outline of 'Akká. We gathered on the terrace until 'Abdu'l-Bahá appeared and entered the Shrine. He generally chanted the Tablet of Visitation, but sometimes He asked Shoghi Effendi to chant it. When it was over and the believers started to come out, He stood at the door with a vial of rosewater and put a little in each one's hand.

I remember following Him as He walked among the pines, past the Holy Shrine on Mt. Carmel, deeply absorbed in thought, while the setting sun came down into the Mediterranean Sea.[33]

'Abdu'l-Bahá and Shoghi Effendi (standing on the far left) with the pilgrims and residents on the terrace overlooking Haifa

'Alí Yazdí's story of a meal (1917):

There were also memorable little details such as eating at the table with 'Abdu'l-Bahá. He ate very simply, but He insisted on others having the proper amount of food. Quite often He would come behind the guests and talk to them. He came behind me and said, "Why aren't you eating?" I was shy; I was hungry, but I did not dare eat. "Why aren't you eating, Sheikh-'Alí?" He would repeat. He would then put a large helping of rice on my plate. I had to eat it![34]

'Alí Yazdí's story of a special meeting (1917):

> One day I was walking back from the business section of
> town. All the streets were winding there, and the roads were
> dirt roads, not macadam. I was going around a curved street
> up the hill toward the house of 'Abdu'l-Bahá. As I turned
> the corner, there He was. I saw 'Abdu'l-Bahá with two of the
> believers behind Him, walking down the hill. As was the cus-
> tom, I stepped to one side and bowed. He stopped and walked
> over to me, right in front of me, and He looked me straight
> in the eyes. That is something I will never forget—looking at
> 'Abdu'l-Bahá face to face.[35]

Bahíyyih Winckler's story of seeing 'Abdu'l-Bahá for the first time
(1919):

> We left town and began to climb upward until the hors-
> es stopped before a wall with a large wrought-iron gate. We
> looked through the bars to see a large stone house in the mid-
> dle of a sandy yard. We were going to stay in this house twelve
> days.
>
> Suddenly it was as if a hand turned my face to the left. I saw
> a window at the top of a small building behind a wall. In the
> upper half of the window was the face of 'Abdu'l-Bahá. He was
> looking at us and yet into some distant place. Without any ac-
> tion on my part, I became close to Him. His eyes were radiant,
> and they spoke of love and wisdom, but there was also a look
> of patient sadness. He did not speak or move. I looked beyond
> Him and saw a large circle of soft pink with a white center. The
> edges of the circle were gray with sparkles of gold. It was very
> beautiful, and I became aware that it was telling me something

about the Master—how wonderful He was—but I did not understand. I did know that His Father, Bahá'u'lláh, had given Him the title "Master" because He must be respected.

Then I was wrapped in a feeling of love towards the Master that flooded my heart. As suddenly as this happened, it was over. Later, after I thought about this unusual incident, I decided it was a gift from the Master. It was a gift that was beyond measure, one that would remain with me forever. It was a gift in two ways: first, it made me realize that the Master's great station was beyond comprehension; and second, it taught me that I could be close to Him if I loved Him.[36]

Bahíyyih Winckler's story of meeting 'Abdu'l-Bahá for the first time (1919):

The home we stayed in proved to be spacious for all of my family. . . . We soon met Shoghi Effendi, 'Abdu'l-Bahá's eldest grandson, who was ten years older than I. He came to greet us and to say that the Master would be coming very soon, and then there 'Abdu'l-Bahá was, in the doorway! I caught my breath, but the Master smiled and welcomed us with enthusiasm. He shook our hands and made us feel He was really glad we had come. We all sat down when He did.

The Master asked us about our trip. No one told Him about the terrible storm we had been through in the Mediterranean. The old ship, which had been out of use for some time and then brought back into service to carry troops during World War I, had groaned and shaken when the huge waves crashed down upon us. The captain had said it was the worst storm he had ever been in. We had been a little frightened, but perhaps the Master knew this and protected us.[37]

*'Abdu'l-Bahá with Bahíyyih Winckler in a photograph taken by
Shoghi Effendi. Also in the photograph are George Latimer, Albert Vail,
Hand of the Cause of God John Esslemont, Harry Randall, Arthur Hathaway,
and Ruth Randall.*

Bahíyyih Winckler's story of visiting the Shrine of the Báb (1919):

> [We] went to a gathering at the Shrine of the Báb, the
> Herald of the Bahá'í Faith. . . . The Shrine of the Báb has
> more than one room, and the Master led us to a door where
> we all took off our shoes. . . . I stood by the Master's side. As
> each person entered the room, the Master put rose water in
> their hands. He had a very small bottle, and I watched. There
> was always enough, even for me at the end. How could it be?
> Maybe it was a miracle. In this room prayers were chanted, but
> I could not understand the words.[38]

Bahíyyih Winckler's story of dinner with the Master (1919):

> To prepare for dinner with the Master, Mother and I put
> on our best dresses. Dinner was at 7:30, and we were on time.

46

Father was never late to anything. He said the Master was the same. Unless there was a reason, I was never allowed to be late.

'Abdu'l-Bahá placed each person at the table. He placed Mother at the head, Father and George partway down, and Shoghi Effendi and Dr. Ḥakím at the far end because they were taking notes of all that the Master said. He placed me at His left side. That was to be my place all during our visit.

Fujita came in carrying large plates of pilaf and other things. The pilaf had dainty pieces of meat and vegetables mixed into the rice, and on top, there were pine nuts. The Master talked a great deal, but never lost sight of anyone's plate. When someone's plate was empty He would arise from His chair and, still talking, fill it. He did this to Father twice, and I knew Father was struggling to eat it all, but no one would leave even a speck. When the Master was silent, no one spoke. There was a loving respect that one could feel. Shoghi Effendi interpreted as the Master spoke, and he did not seem to have time to eat very much.[39]

Bahíyyih Winckler's story of speaking with the Master (1919):

The Master always spoke to me in English and did so with the others when He wished to.[40]

Bahíyyih Winckler's story of a private meeting (1919):

When Shoghi Effendi came in the morning, he said that the Master would give us each a private interview. Mother's would be in the morning. I was a little afraid to have mine for fear I would cry or say something silly. To be alone with the Master would not be an ordinary experience. Mother said I could go with her, so we hurried along. It was pouring rain. The Master greeted us in His loving way by putting both hands to His forehead. He took us to the room where He held meetings and received guests, seated us, and then sat down across from us. I called this room the "meeting room."

Mother had lots to say. . . . Then it was my turn. I stood up and asked (I heard this coming out of my mouth, with surprise), "What can I do to serve the Faith?" There was a long silence, and then I heard, "Study, study, STUDY." When the Master wanted to emphasize something, He would repeat it three times, His voice getting louder and louder.[41]

Bahíyyih Winckler's story of receiving her new name (1919):

At luncheon the Master turned to me, saying, "Your name is 'Bahíyyih.' It means light, and there must be something to make the light." He had a twinkle in His eyes and a big smile. I loved the name at once. It had a soft, musical sound. "Margaret," the name my parents gave me, had a harsh sound, and I had never liked it. Later, I learned the name Bahíyyih was the name of the sister of 'Abdu'l-Bahá, the Greatest Holy Leaf. . . . I am sure the Master heard my heart saying thank you.[42]

Bahíyyih Winckler's stories of luncheons (1919):

Luncheons continued to be brought to us from the Master's house. Shoghi Effendi and Dr. Ḥakím were always with us, and sometimes Dr. Esslemont was, too. The wonderful surprise was that on this day the Master came, saying that He would be with us every day. Shoghi Effendi assured us that this was a great honor because 'Abdu'l-Bahá seldom had time to do this. The big table with the white cloth was made beautiful when the Master took fragrant jasmine blossoms from a large handkerchief in His pocket and tossed them into the center of the table.

The Master was always so happy, even when one day He was terribly tired, having had only four hours of sleep and no breakfast. We became like a family, feeling free to laugh and ask questions, but always with respect. . . .[43]

The luncheons were our happiest times because the Master was so jolly. I kept thinking about this because we had grown so close to Him. . . .[44]

Luncheon [on another] day was especially fun. The Master encouraged Fujita to try to teach Him to eat rice with chopsticks. We all laughed, even the Master. . . .[45]

[One day] it was raining again. At noon time it came down in sheets, but the Master came for lunch just the same. He sat with us, not as a wise man who can accomplish anything, but as someone who was part of our lives.[46]

The Master teased me about food during the entire visit. He would ask if I liked something that was being served. If I said "A little," He would usually say, "I know what you are thinking." And the next day, for me, we would have chicken and potatoes, and it tasted good! Another time, we had a delicious sweet that looked like pink shredded wheat, only it was very brittle. It was a real treat. He was so kind and thoughtful.[47]

Bahíyyih Winckler's story of learning obedience (1919):

Our dessert was a dish of fresh dates. I had tasted them in Cairo and had decided never to eat them or yogurt again. . . . The Master put two dates on a little plate in front of me and explained that they helped the digestion and gave heat

49

to the body. Then He arose from the table and left us. We always went to the door to watch Him walk home. After He left, I turned to the dining room table and saw it had been cleared. I was thankful, for the dates were gone. But in the corner of the room was another table with the dates on it, and they were looking at me! I stood on one foot and then the other. Must I eat those dates? Every reason not to came into my mind. I discovered one date was a little rotten, so of course it would not be necessary to eat that one. But something also kept saying to me, The Master told you to. The Master never asks you to do something unless it is for your own good. After about ten minutes I ate both dates. I felt heroic, wise, and relieved.[48]

. . . During dinner the Master turned to me, saying, "Yogurt is very good." He turned to Fujita and asked him to get some for me. Fujita went to get some yogurt but returned at once, saying there was none and should he go next door? The Master said, "No, that is not necessary." Then He looked at me with such a kind look. This is what had happened to me. When the Master had said yogurt, I had reacted in only one way—instant obedience. I did not remember that I had decided never even to smell it again. The Master had shown me, in a way I could understand, what obedience means. When God speaks through His chosen channels—His Teachers—for your own good and happiness, do not question it. This was yet another gift from the Master that I had needed. It was a basic lesson for a lifetime.[49]

Bahíyyih Winckler's story of going to the Shrine of the Báb (1919):

That afternoon, we all went to the Shrine of the Báb. A carriage took some of us up over the awful rocky road. . . . A few minutes after we arrived, 'Abdu'l-Bahá came and stood, looking at the sea. He told us that someday the drive to 'Akká and the Shrine of Bahá'u'lláh would be beautiful with orange groves. A great breakwater would be built to form a harbor, and ships from all over the world would come. The Shrine of the Báb would be lighted and would be a landmark for ships and airplanes. He turned to the Shrine and stood by the door of the large room. I stood next to Him as He gave everyone a little rose water. It was the same story as before—the little bottle that never got empty. It was more than I could understand. We went to the room where the Báb's body lies. Shoghi Effendi chanted the Tablet of Visitation. There is something in the Shrines that one's heart responds to. Then the carriage was waiting to take us down the hill.[50]

'Azíz Yazdí explains his vivid recollections (1919–1921):

> . . . my recollections are the recollections of a child between the ages of nine and twelve. But there are so many incidents that remain so clear in my mind because the personality of 'Abdu'l-Bahá is such that you don't forget. It stays with you, it stays with you, it has its imprint in your heart and soul, and you always would turn to Him, and He's there living in front of you, and you can talk to Him and get inspiration from Him. So the few memories I have and recollections are living, they are not just old memories. I can never forget them, and every time I think of them and talk about them, it's as if I was living them, really.[51]

'Azíz Yazdí remembers the Sunday meetings (1919–1921):

> . . . every Sunday there was a meeting on Mount Carmel in the room which is now the resting place of 'Abdu'l-Bahá; it

is next to the resting place of the Báb. And the meeting took place there, and 'Abdu'l-Bahá attended this meeting, and He spoke. First of all He used to ask [a] few of the friends to say prayers, and then He spoke to us. It was such wonderful moments, really, to be in His presence. You know as if you are in heaven, in the presence of God himself, almost, almost. He spoke to us about the progress of the Faith all over the world, about the future of Haifa and of 'Akká. . . . And 'Abdu'l-Bahá used to admonish us, give us wonderful talks. He was so kind to everyone.

And then at the end of the meeting He led the way to where the Báb is buried, which is the Shrine of the Báb, and it was customary that He stood at the gate with a bottle of rosewater in His hand, and often next to Him there was a prominent Bahá'í who came from overseas. And we went one by one after taking our shoes off, stretched our hand, and He put a few drops of this rosewater with His blessed hand on our hand, and we spread this all over ourselves as much as possible to be blessed by it. And then we entered the Shrine of the Báb. . . .

'Abdu'l-Bahá was the last one to come in, and His coming in was something that—a picture that I never forget. It was with such humility that when He reached the threshold, He went down on His knees, He put His forehead on the threshold, and you could see the love, the humility He had for the Báb. It really tears one's heart to see such devotion, such love. What a sight! And then He got up and chanted the Tablet of Visitation, and His voice was heavenly, beautiful. It just goes into your heart and lifts you up to different spheres in life, different areas in life. And then He went out, and that was the end of that particular meeting.

This took place every Sunday.[52]

'Abdu'l-Bahá walking with the pilgrims on the slopes of Mount Carmel

'Azíz Yazdí's story of the Master lovingly remembering his brother and mother (1919–1921):

> . . . the Nineteen Day Feast took place again in the same room where the Sunday meetings took place. Again the Master asked people to say prayers, and then He spoke to us. [A]t the end of the meeting, there was a big table with refreshments and things that were tied in tissue handkerchiefs in a big tray. [W]e came one by one, and the Beloved Master with His own hand gave us one of these, and we went out and ate it.
>
> I remember once my younger brother did not come because he was sick. I just wanted you to listen to this to see how thoughtful 'Abdu'l-Bahá is. So when my turn came, I received my share, and I kissed it, and I was going out to eat it and enjoy it, and the Beloved Master stopped me and gave me another one and said, "This is for your brother who is sick." So you can imagine my joy and my happiness! I wanted to run and tell my father "Look, 'Abdu'l-Bahá remembered my little

brother!" You know we were very small. He stopped me again and gave me a third one and said. "This is for your mother who stayed home to look after your brother."

Now this is a lesson for all of us. . . . A little child [was] sick [and was] not [able to] come. 'Abdu'l-Bahá remembered![53]

'Azíz Yazdí's story of getting extra gifts (1919–1921):

Once as a child—you know children are naughty—I knew that in the kitchen of the Master's house there were some good things. . . . And I came to the House of the Master and I looked around. There was no one there. And there was a big hall, so I ran across the hall to go to the kitchen. And halfway through I heard the voice of the Master calling me. I knew that I am going to be punished. So I stood there not moving at all until the Beloved Master came near me. And instead of punishing me, he stroked my head, my cheek, gave me an apple and some money, and then said, "Now you can go to the kitchen." What can you do, it is so beautiful, so lovely. . . . There are many such instances you know, many such instances.[54]

'Azíz Yazdí's story of going to the Shrine of Bahá'u'lláh with the Master (1919–1921):

One day I was in Bahjí playing in the gardens, and the Beloved Master came out of the pilgrim house. I bowed with reverence. He looked at me, smiled, and walked towards the Shrine of Bahá'u'lláh. I don't know what came over me, but I had a feeling of a power pulling me towards 'Abdu'l-Bahá. And I followed Him. I am certain he knew I was following Him, but He never turned back to look at me or to tell me not to. I

'Abdu'l-Bahá walking up Haparsim Street. The children are eating the sweets that 'Abdu'l-Bahá just gave them.

continued following Him until He reached the entrance to the Shrine of Bahá'u'lláh. I was still behind Him. He went in, and I followed Him. I remember exactly the spot where He stood and went on His knees in front of the Shrine of Bahá'u'lláh. And then He got up and chanted the Tablet of Visitation. The distance between the Beloved Master and myself was about four to five yards, not more, but when the voice of the Beloved Master was heard first, something happened and I asked myself, "Where am I? In this Holy Spot, here is the Qiblih where Bahá'u'lláh lies and here is the Beloved Master chanting the Tablet of Visitation. I am the only one witnessing that. This is nothing but the grace, the bounty and generosity of 'Abdu'l-Bahá."[55]

Sylvia Paine's story of meeting 'Abdu'l-Bahá (1920):

He came in like a ray of light and life. He sat down at the end of the table, bade us be seated. . . . The Master said that He hoped we were well and very happy. Then He asked again if we were well.

Mrs. Paine said, "We are all very well except Sylvia, who was a little ill in the night, but that is not serious."

'Abdu'l-Bahá replied: "I hope she will soon be well."

Sylvia smiled and nodded and the Master said, "That will soon pass away and you will be well again." Then he continued, "Your food and rooms are very simple here, but your purpose in coming here makes them seem good to you."[56]

Sylvia Paine's story of getting a new name (1920):

. . . The Master . . . gave Sylvia a Bahá'í name, Badí'a, which means "something new and wonderful." We were not present

*'Abdu'l-Bahá in the garden He planted outside the
Shrine of Bahá'u'lláh at Bahjí*

when he gave her the name, but Mabel said that he walked up
and down the room, radiating power and love.

When Sylvia came back with her new name, the Holy Mother
brought out a box of candy, in honor of Sylvia's nameday. The
candy was white with a little chocolate center. Bringing it out
in Sylvia's honor was one of the sweetest, kindest acts of simple

thoughtfulness that we saw in Haifa. Needless to say, Sylvia Badí'a Paine was a very happy girl that day. . . .

He shook hands with us in parting. When He said goodbye to Sylvia, He smiled down at her and said, "Sylvia!—Badí'a Khánum!—Miss Badí'a!" and His voice was filled with the most affectionate and sweet laughter![57]

'Abdu'l-Bahá

Sylvia Paine remembers the Master's voice (1920):

When we had the final evening and before we left, I remember so clearly how He spoke to me and He said "Sylvia Badí'a! Very good! Khaylí khúb!" . . . and He said it in this wonderful voice. His voice I think made more impression on me than any other one thing about being with Him. It was the most beautiful musical voice, strong and full, with rich overtones and I remember thinking on that last evening if I could just carry the feeling, the memory, of that voice in my mind for the rest of my life I would be happy.[58]

Stories about Shoghi Effendi as a Child

Shoghi Effendi

A special name bestowed upon a special grandson (1897):

> . . . it was this oldest one who bore witness to the saying "the child is the secret essence of its sire," not to be taken to mean in this case the heritage of his own father, but rather that he was sired by the Prophets of God and inherited the nobility of

his Grandfather 'Abdu'l-Bahá. The depths of 'Abdu'l-Bahá's feelings at this time are reflected in His own words in which He clearly states that the name Shoghi—literally "the one who longs"—was conferred by God upon this grandson:

> . . . O God! This is a branch sprung from the tree of Thy mercy. Through Thy grace and bounty enable him to grow and through the showers of Thy generosity cause him to become a verdant, flourishing, blossoming and fruitful branch. Gladden the eyes of his parents, Thou Who giveth to whomsoever Thou willest, and bestow upon him the name Shoghi so that he may yearn for Thy Kingdom and soar into the realms of the unseen![1]

The title "Effendi" or Sir, added as a term of respect, is an integral part of Shoghi Effendi's name. The Master required everyone, including Shoghi Effendi's own father, to add the title Effendi to the name and always to address him as Shoghi Effendi. . . . The surname "Rabbání" which means "divine," was conferred upon him by the Master. . . .[2]

The first time the Bahá'ís see Shoghi Effendi (1897):

> . . . I heard the whisper that from the sacred lineage [of Bahá'u'lláh], a new babe had been born and had been named Shoghi Effendi. . . . For some time the residents of the pilgrim house had shown great interest in seeing Shoghi Effendi; they pleaded continually with [his father] in the hope that such longing by so many might be realized. Quite by

chance one day, this Babe of only four months was brought to the bírúní of 'Abdu'l-Bahá's house. There friends were beside themselves with joy and I, too, hastened to pay a visit to that beloved Infant. But I made every effort to look at him in no other light than as a Bahá'í child. However, a strong urge compelled me to bow my head and observe the deepest respect. For about a minute I was utterly captivated by the beauty of that face. I gently kissed the soft hair of his blessed head, and as I did so I felt an indescribable quality in that Infant. I could see his likeliness to the pictures that I had seen of the infant Jesus in the arms of His mother Mary. For several days an image of His shining face was before my eyes, but gradually it faded.[3]

Hearing the chanting of the Qur'án (1897):

The childhood nurse of Shoghi Effendi used to recount that when he was still a baby the Master was wont to call one of the Muslims who chanted in the mosque to come at least once a week and chant to the child, in his melodious voice, the sublime verses of the Qur'án.[4]

Vivid and significant dreams (1897):

Shoghi Effendi was sometimes subject to vivid and significant dreams, both pleasant and unpleasant. It is reported that in his babyhood he woke one night crying and the Master told his nurse to bring Shoghi Effendi to Him so that He could comfort him; the Master said to His sister, the Greatest Holy Leaf, "See, already he has dreams!"[4]

A parrot calls his name:

> . . . in the house of 'Abdu'lláh Pá<u>sh</u>á there used to be a parrot. The Greatest Holy Leaf used to take a mirror, hold it before the bird and bid it to say "Ya Ilahi va Mahbubi" (O my God and my Beloved!) and to say "Shoghi jan!" (Shoghi dear!) Early in the morning, at dawn . . . the household could hear the parrot crying "Ya Ilahi va Mahbubi! Shoghi jan!" . . . with its high pitch.[5]

The first to attend morning prayers (1899):

> In those days of Shoghi Effendi's childhood it was the custom to rise about dawn and spend the first hour of the day in the Master's room, where prayers were said and the family all had breakfast with Him. The children sat on the floor, their legs folded under them, their arms folded across their breasts, in great respect; when asked they would chant for 'Abdu'l-Bahá; there was no shouting or unseemly conduct. Breakfast consisted of tea, brewed on the bubbling Russian brass samovar and served in little crystal glasses, very hot and very sweet, pure wheat bread and goats' milk cheese. . . . Shoghi Effendi was always the first to get up and be on time. . . .[6]

Greeting the Master (1899):

> One of the youngest members of the family made a special mark on Ella [Goodall]'s heart—'Abdu'l-Bahá's eldest grandchild, Shoghi Effendi, who had just passed his second birthday. She described the toddler in a letter to her mother as "a perfect little picture and reminds me of the Old Mas-

ter's [sic] children in the pictures." This child had been born at the House of 'Abdu'lláh Páshá during March of 1897 to the Master's eldest daughter and her husband, a relative of the Báb, making him the physical embodiment of the mystical connection between the two Divine Messengers. One memory of that little boy especially stood out in Ella's mind and she wrote about it years later at the time Shoghi Effendi became his Grandfather's successor as Head of the Faith, that is, assumed the role of Guardian.

One day . . . I had joined the ladies of the Family in the room of the Greatest Holy Leaf for early morning tea, the beloved Master was sitting in His favourite corner of the divan where, through the window on His right, He could look over the ramparts and see the blue Mediterranean beyond. He was busy writing Tablets, and the quiet peace of the room was broken only by the bubble of the samovar, where one of the young maidservants, sitting on the floor before it, was brewing the tea.

. . . a small figure appeared in the open doorway, directly opposite 'Abdu'l-Bahá. Having dropped off his shoes he stepped into the room, with his eyes focused on the Master's face. 'Abdu'l-Bahá returned his gaze with such a look of loving welcome it seemed to beckon the small one to approach Him. Shoghi, that beautiful little boy, with his exquisite cameo face and his soulful appealing dark eyes, walked slowly toward the divan, the Master drawing him as by an invisible thread, until he stood quite close in front of Him. As he paused there a moment 'Abdu'l-Bahá did not offer to embrace but sat perfectly still, only nodding His head two or three times, slowly and impressively, as if

Shoghi Effendi

to say—"You see? This tie connecting us is not just that of a physical grandfather but something far deeper and more significant." While we breathlessly watched to see what he would do, the little boy reached down and picking up the hem of 'Abdu'l-Bahá's robe he touched it reverently to his forehead, and kissed it, then gently replaced it, while never taking his eyes from the adored Master's face. The next moment he turned away, and scampered off to play, like any normal child. . . .[7]

64

Chanting in a slightly sleepy voice:

> A gentle breeze blew through the blinds, and beyond them
> [were] the green vineyards of Mount Carmel, spread out in the
> morning sun. Alone, at the head of the room on a divan, sat
> the Greatest Holy Leaf. Regal and yet at the same time self-
> effacing, she wore the graceful flowing headscarf and garments
> of the East. Another divan ran the length of the room under
> the many windows, and at its head, at the right hand upper
> corner and near His sister, sat 'Abdu'l-Bahá. Halfway down
> from the Master was His consort, Munírih Khánum. . . . At
> the further, the "lower," end of the room were little boys and
> girls of the Household, and from time to time one or another
> child would sweetly chant. . . . one grandchild, Shoghi Effendi,
> [was] chanting in a slightly sleepy voice that reminded [one] of
> the dawn chirpings of awakening birds.[8]

A mischievous child:

> It may sound disrespectful to say the Guardian was a mis-
> chievous child, but he himself told me he was the acknowledged
> ringleader of all the other children. Bubbling with high spirits,
> enthusiasm and daring, full of laughter and wit, the small boy
> led the way in many pranks; whenever something was afoot,
> behind it would be found Shoghi Effendi! The boundless en-
> ergy was often a source of anxiety as he would rush madly up
> and down the long flight of high steps to the upper story of
> the house, to the consternation of the pilgrims below, waiting
> to meet the Master. His exuberance was irrepressible and was
> in the child the same force that was to make the man such an
> untiring and unflinching commander-in-chief of the forces of

Bahá'u'lláh leading them to victory after victory, indeed, to the spiritual conquest of the entire globe. We have a very reliable witness to this characteristic of the Guardian, 'Abdu'l-Bahá Himself, Who wrote on a used envelope a short sentence to please His little Grandson: "Shoghi Effendi is a wise man—but he runs about very much!"

It must not be inferred, however, that Shoghi Effendi was mannerless. Children in the East—how much more the chil-

Shoghi Effendi with Western believers on pilgrimage in 1901

dren of 'Abdu'l-Bahá—were taught courtesy and manners from the cradle. Bahá'u'lláh's family was descended from kings and the family tradition, entirely apart from His divine teachings which enjoin courtesy as obligatory, ensured that a noble conduct and politeness would distinguish Shoghi Effendi from his babyhood.[9]

Obedience (1902):

... when Shoghi Effendi was only five years old he was pestering the Master to write something for him, whereupon 'Abdu'l-Bahá wrote this touching and revealing letter in His own hand:

He is God!

O My Shoghi, I have no time to talk, leave me alone! You said "write"—I have written. What else should be done? Now is not the time for you to read and write, it is the time for jumping about and chanting "O my God!", therefore memorize the prayers of the Blessed Beauty and chant them that I may hear them, because there is no time for anything else.

It seems that when this wonderful gift reached the child he set himself to memorize a number of Bahá'u'lláh's prayers and would chant them so loudly that the entire neighbourhood could hear his voice; when his parents and other members of the Master's family remonstrated with him, Shoghi Effendi replied . . . , "The Master wrote to me to chant that He may hear me! I am doing my best!" and he kept on chanting at the top of his voice for many hours every day. Finally his parents begged the Master to stop him, but He told them to let Shoghi Effendi alone. This was one aspect of the small boy's chanting. We are told there was another: he had memorized some touching passages written by 'Abdu'l-Bahá after the ascension of Bahá'u'lláh and when he chanted these the tears would roll down the earnest little face. From another source we are told that when the Master was requested by a western friend, at that time living in His home, to reveal a prayer for children He did so, and the first to memorize it and chant it was Shoghi Effendi who would also chant it in the meetings of the friends.[10]

A desire to learn:

. . . one day Shoghi Effendi entered the Master's room, took up His pen and tried to write. 'Abdu'l-Bahá drew him to His side, tapped him gently on the shoulder and said "Now is not the time to write, now is the time to play, you will write a lot in the future." Nevertheless the desire of the child to learn led to the formation of classes in the Master's household for the children, taught by an old Persian believer. I know that at one time in his childhood, most likely while he was still living in 'Akká, Shoghi Effendi and other grandchildren were taught by an Italian, who acted as governess or teacher.[11]

Going to school:

[Haji Mírzá Ḥaydar 'Alí] was asked by the Master to teach the children of His household. . . . Shoghi Effendi . . . was among his students. Ḥaydar 'Alí recognized his station even at this early age. Whenever the young Shoghi Effendi would enter the class, Haji Mírzá Ḥaydar 'Alí would rise in respect for his student. He often whispered in his ear, "Sufficient to you is the school of the Master."[12]

"I need him":

> We are told that sometimes he spent the night in Bahjí in the house now used as a pilgrim house; 'Abdu'l-Bahá would Himself come and tuck him in bed, remarking "I need him."[13]

A treat for a favorite grandchild:

> . . . what the grandchildren used to watch for was the mouthful of <u>Kh</u>ánum [the Greatest Holy Leaf's] food that she would give to this or that one as it always tasted best. They called it "the mouthful of <u>Kh</u>ánum"; the Guardian usually got it as he was a favorite of hers![14]

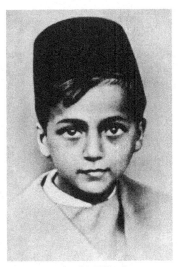

Shoghi Effendi

Following his Grandfather (1904–1905):

Shoghi Effendi was at the time a child of seven or eight years of age. He was rather small for his age, but very keen and attentive. When not engaged in his early morning studies, he followed his Grandfather ['Abdu'l-Bahá] wherever He went. He was almost like His shadow and passed long hours seated on the rug in the manner of the East, listening, quietly and silently, to every word He uttered. The child had a remark-ably retentive memory and, at times when guests were present, the Master would ask him either to recite some passage from Bahá'u'lláh's Writings, which he had memorized, or to chant a prayer. It was very moving to hear the limpid, crystal chanting of that child, because all his being and soul were engaged in communion with God. Eagerness was ever present and animat-ed him like a flame of fire in all he did.[15]

Praying with rapt adoration (1906):

During the visit to the Tomb of Bahá'u'lláh, the figure of a boy was kneeling in rapt adoration, and the thought passed through my mind, "What destiny lies before this boy . . .?" It was Shoghi Effendi, who, by his Grandfather's will, has been, at the age of 24, made leader of the Movement.[16]

Taking care of the pilgrims from an early age (1906):

. . . Along toward evening, they had driven up Mount Car-mel for their last visit to the Tomb of the Báb. They were on their way back down the mountain when suddenly out of the shadows there appeared Shoghi Effendi, oldest grandson of

'Abdu'l-Bahá. The child had prevailed on his tutor to let him ride down the mountain on his donkey from their summer home and meet [their] carriage for a last goodbye.[17]

A significant dream (1907):

Although there is no doubt that 'Abdu'l-Bahá did every-thing to ensure Shoghi Effendi had as happy and carefree a childhood as possible, it must have been out of the question to hide from so sensitive and intelligent a child the fact that great dangers threatened his beloved Grandfather in those years immediately preceding the overthrow of the Sulṭán of Turkey.

Perhaps because of this situation, constantly worsening, 'Abdu'l-Bahá sent Shoghi Effendi to live in Haifa with his nurse, where already some of the believers resided . . . French was his first foreign language . . . [Shoghi Effendi entered the best school in Haifa, the College des Freres, conducted by the Jesuits.] By 1907 he was living with this same nurse, Hájar Khátún, who had always been with him from his infancy, in the newly constructed house of 'Abdu'l-Bahá, which became His last home and later the home of the Guardian. It was here that Shoghi Effendi had a very significant dream which he recounted. . . . He said that when he was nine or ten years old, living with his nurse in this house and attending school in Haifa, he dreamed that he and another child, an Arab school-mate, were in the room in which 'Abdu'l-Bahá used to receive His guests in the house in 'Akká, where the Master was living and where Shoghi Effendi had been born. The Báb entered the room and then a man with a revolver appeared and shot at the Báb; then he told Shoghi Effendi "Now it is your turn" and began to chase him around the room to shoot him. At this

Shoghi Effendi woke up. He repeated this dream to his nurse, who told him to tell it to Mírzá Asadu'lláh and ask him to tell the Master. Mírzá Asadu'lláh wrote it all down and sent it to the Master Who replied by revealing for Shoghi Effendi this Tablet. The strange thing, Shoghi Effendi said, is that it was just about this time that 'Abdu'l-Bahá was in great danger and wrote one of His Wills in which He appointed Shoghi Effendi as Guardian.

He is God!

Shoghi Mine

This dream is a very good one. Rest assured that to have attained the presence of His Holiness the Exalted One, may my soul be a sacrifice to Him, is a proof of receiving the grace of God and obtaining His most great bounty and supreme favour. The same is true of the rest of the dream. It is my hope that you may manifest the outpourings of the Abhá Beauty and wax day by day in faith and knowledge. At night pray and supplicate and in the day do what is required of you.

'Abdu'l-Bahá[18]

The joy of his visits:

So often it was ten at night before the Beloved One had His little supper which the Greatest Holy Leaf, His dear sister would try to keep warm on the brazier in her room, and by the way that room was open for all in the household. Guests were received in

Shoghi Effendi

the tea room but all the family and servants of both sexes were free to come to this haven of refuge at any time. Part of the room was higher than the rest and the modest and humble generally sat on the step where the division came. All around the windows was a raised seat with cushions and the family usually sat there. At times the Beloved One came there too . . .

It was this room that the children flocked to. And I shall never forget our beloved Guardian when as a little boy home from his holidays from the monastery school on Mount Carmel was graphically describing to her whom he so loved all his experiences during his absence from her, and she loving him equally seemed to hang onto his words. He stood on the bed

73

and emphasized his tale with the gesticulations he had probably caught from the French in the monastery. It is a sweet picture often before me.

And speaking of the beloved Guardian I may tell you that these visits were the joy of all the young people as well as for the older members. For days before his coming there was an excitement in the air and great preparations. Then when he came he took hold of himself and with his splendid initiative kept the ball rolling and household amused and entertained during his stay.

As there was a dramatic element at the monastery school so he felt there should be in the holy household, and he drew up a poster which was placed in the hall. I never saw the theatricals but I can imagine that they were stage-managed. Then he held a banquet or feast rather in the servants quarters for all the young people, and I am told it was beautifully arranged with little paper napkins and flowers at each place. I wish I could remember more about those delightful but fleeting visits. I only know that they meant everything to the little people, and I am sure to his dear mother and the Beloved and to the Greatest Holy Leaf.[19]

Respectful in the presence of his Grandfather (1908):

‘Abdu’l-Bahá’s eldest grandson . . . entered and kissed the Master’s hand. . . . While his Grandfather and father conversed, young Shoghi Effendi greeted the ladies, and then waited respectfully near the door. (The door in many Eastern countries is the “lower” part of the room. Here is the “shoe-row,” where, traditionally, shoes are left on entering. Here the attendants may wait. The point farthest from the “shoe-row” is the “highest” part of the room.) Several Persian gentlemen then entered the room, and about a quarter of an hour was "spent in leave-taking and in greetings," and comings and go-ings. [Shoghi Effendi] . . . was dressed in a European summer suit—a short jacket and short trousers but with long stockings reaching above the knee. He seemed to be eleven or twelve, she later wrote, and what struck her in the young face was "the dark, early advanced, yes even melancholy eyes." The boy stood motionless "in his respectful, expectant bearing and posture." Then, the room emptying, he slowly approached his beloved Grandfather and waited for Him to speak, then replied diffidently in Persian, then was dismissed with a smile and, not permitted this time to kiss the Master's hand, backed respectfully out of the room, all the time . . . keeping "his dark, true-hearted eyes steadily on the blue, magic glances of his Grandfather."[20]

The scholar is told to sleep:

> While attending school in Beirut, Shoghi Effendi spent his vacations in Haifa, often in a small room next to the room occupied by 'Abdu'l-Bahá. He would spend hours studying and reading. At times his lamp remained turned on late at night, and the Master would get up and go to his door, saying "Enough! Enough! Go to sleep!"[21]

The special relationship with the Greatest Holy Leaf (1914):

> The school holidays began and the children of the household returned from Beirut. Shoghi Effendi also returned to Haifa to spend the holidays. When the Greatest Holy Leaf took Shoghi Effendi in her arms her eyes lit up with joy. I realized that the love was reciprocated. Shoghi Effendi looked very frail and

Shoghi Effendi

weak. The Greatest Holy Leaf inquired, "Why are you so weak: See how the other youth are fit and wholesome." He replied, "I don't like the food there and can't eat it." The Greatest Holy Leaf said, "Then how is it that others seem to like the food and eat it?" He replied, "They are able to spend more money and can eat better food." The behaviour and quality of this young man was very different from the rest. His friends would play and joke around, but he would rarely take part. He would either be reading a book or a newspaper. His chair would be close to that of the Greatest Holy Leaf and he would spend many of his free hours in this room listening to her, totally absorbed by her fascinating talk. Shoghi Effendi possessed a handsome face, sad and elegant with a sweet, heart-warming and spontaneous smile which on occasion would turn into reverberating laughter.[22]

A spartan life:

The spartan life lived within the limitations imposed upon 'Abdu'l-Baha and His family by a relentless foe had tempered the character of the young Shoghi Effendi who, in becoming accustomed to privations on the one hand, rejoiced in the satisfaction of self-imposed discipline on the other. This quality of thrift in non-essentials remained one of his sterling habits, which permitted him to demonstrate his generosity in all its nobility on matters which reflected upon the greatness of the Cause of God.[23]

'Abdu'l-Bahá with Shoghi Effendi

Stories with the Beloved Guardian
Shoghi Effendi

Shoghi Effendi

Badíʻ Bushrúʼíʼs story of being with Shoghi Effendi (1902):

> The blessing of being a child drew the attention of Shoghi
> Effendi towards this insignificant being and I was called "the
> little traveler." Most of the time, be it during playtime or vis-

its to the Shrine of Bahá'u'lláh, I was privileged to be in his presence.[1]

Bahíyyih Winckler's story of taking a photograph of Shoghi Effendi (1919):

> Shoghi Effendi was also in the garden. He had a grapefruit in his hands. I asked if I could take his picture, and he said yes. He was such a smiling, kind person. He was completely devoted to his Grandfather, working day and night with Him.[2]

Bahíyyih Winckler's story of visiting the Garden of Riḍván (1919):

> We left the barracks and met the carriages so we could be taken to the Riḍván Gardens. . . . The garden was surrounded by a stream, like an island. I would call it a brook. We crossed a short bridge and entered a place of flowers and fruit. It was November, and yet the garden looked so fresh and happy.
>
> The gardener came to talk to us. He pointed out special plants, some of which had been carried all the way from Persia by pilgrims, some of whom had walked the entire distance. He went to the mulberry trees that shaded the bench where Bahá'u'lláh used to sit, sometimes resting and other times dictating important Tablets.
>
> A table was set up near the trees for lunch, and we enjoyed a delicious pilaf. The dessert was fruit from the garden: oranges, dates, lemons, pomegranates, and watermelon. It was truly a very special garden. The little fountain near where we were sitting was not working. I wanted to see it flowing, because that would make it like the days when Bahá'u'lláh was there.

Shoghi Effendi

The gardener took us to a corner of the property where a fence enclosed a round dirt track. A donkey was standing there. The donkey, when harnessed and blindfolded (the donkey would not walk until it was blindfolded), would walk round and round the track, and the water would begin to flow. The fountain came alive, making a soft sound. How cool it must have been to sit beside the fountain on a hot day. It was selfish of me to ask, but it was so lovely, and we all enjoyed it.

81

After lunch we were taken to the little building where Bahá'u'lláh used to rest and have tea. It had not changed. His room was at the top of a short flight of stairs, and below was where the gardener lived. In this garden, one feels close to Bahá'u'lláh, perhaps because He loved it.[3]

Bahíyyih Winckler's story of visiting the Shrine of Bahá'u'lláh (1919):

We were now going to enter the Shrine of Bahá'u'lláh. . . . First we went through a small garden the Master had made, and then we went through a large door. We took off our shoes. Shoghi Effendi gave us rose water for our faces, then we stopped inside a large room with a small garden in the center. It was raised above the floor level and had a glass roof over it. The floor was covered with beautiful Persian rugs. After a few minutes of silent prayer, Shoghi Effendi chanted the Tablet of Visitation, a special prayer to be said at the Shrine. It was so spiritual. . . . We stood silently. I could not even think. I just felt great peace and power, as if nature also stood still in that room.[4]

'Alí Nakhjavání's story of shaking hands with the Beloved Guardian (1926):

Once our mother asked my brother and I to go to the Master's house after prayers at the Shrine of the Báb. In those days the Guardian was younger and, following prayers, he would walk down to Abbas Street and, the terraces beyond Abbas Street not yet having been built, he would turn to the right on Abbas Street, and then proceed to Haparsim Street

Shoghi Effendi leading pilgrims to the Mansion of Bahjí.
Bahíyyih Winckler is running ahead.

and straight down to the Master's house. The pilgrims would usually walk with him. On that particular day my brother and I, too, followed Shoghi Effendi because we thought how much better it was to go to the Master's house with him. When Shoghi Effendi reached the gate he turned and said, "Fi Amani'llah" (May you be under God's protection) and went in. Being younger than Jalal, I was glad to follow him when he set out after Shoghi Effendi.

The Guardian went up the stairs and we did too, and then entered the house. It was the custom of the Guardian to have his one major meal each day with the Greatest Holy Leaf. It was also his practice to go to her after meeting with the pilgrims and sit and talk to her. Shoghi Effendi turned right to go through the corridor next to the room in which the Master passed away and proceeded to the next room which was the Greatest Holy Leaf's bedroom. He went along that corridor and we followed, and when he opened the door I was so close to Shoghi Effendi at that point that I saw that the Greatest Holy Leaf was in bed.

As soon as she heard the footsteps of Shoghi Effendi and the opening of the door she was at the point of rising from bed to sit in the presence of the Guardian. Although the distance is not far from the door to the bed, Shoghi Effendi literally ran from the door to the bed and gently restrained her, saying "Ja'iz nist" (it is not permissible). He did not want her to be disturbed. . . .

In the room of Khánum [the Greatest Holy Leaf], Shoghi Effendi seated himself. My brother and I, with childish aplomb, sat down too. Then my mother found out what had happened and sent the maid immediately to tell us to come out. The door was opened again and with a motion of her eyes the maid signaled us to leave.

Jalal very reverently stood and bowed and withdrew from the room. But I thought this wasn't right; I thought, "This is not the way to do things!" I felt there should be a handshake. This, of course, was totally inappropriate but to my childish mind it seemed the proper thing to do.

I went straight over to Shoghi Effendi who was seated in a deep comfortable armchair and offered him my little hand. Shoghi Effendi looked at me and pulled himself closer, accepted my hand and shook it. This all took time.

When I went outside my mother asked me what had delayed me and I explained that my brother didn't shake hands and I thought I should. She was horrified and struck my hand, saying, "Out of reverence for the Guardian you should have done exactly what your brother did." Of course, I felt very bad about this. As we were going home my mother asked again, incredulously, "You shook hands?" I said, "Yes." "With your right hand?" "Of course." "Give me your hand." I did, and she kissed it several times.[5]

Amín Banání's story of the Beloved Guardian's heavenly chanting (1934):

> . . . The building known as the Old Eastern Pilgrim House by the Shrine of the Báb . . . was for men in those days, and women were housed in rooms in the house adjacent to the House of 'Abdu'l-Bahá. . . . I at the age of seven and a half . . . could stay either with my father or with my mother. . . .

Shoghi Effendi with the Greatest Holy Leaf

By staying during the day with my father, I could be there when Shoghi Effendi came to see the Eastern men pilgrims every day, and by spending the nights with my mother, I could be there [on] some nights when Shoghi Effendi called the women back to the House of the Master to spend time with them. . . .

Now with the men he came usually about four o'clock in the afternoon to the Shrine, to the entrance by the Shrine, and of course all [the] men were waiting for him, standing outside the pilgrim house. And he would arrive from his house and we would greet him, and then he would proceed to walk on Mount Carmel, and everyone [walked] behind him, . . . and he would talk, and once in a while he would stop and turn back and ask someone a question. . . . At the end of these walks he would come back to the Shrines, that is the Shrine of the Báb and the Shrine of 'Abdu'l-Bahá, which are adjacent. . . .

He himself would remove his shoes, as we would all, and he would stand at the entrance of the Shrine with a container of rosewater. And [to] each one of us, as we entered, he offered some rosewater. We cupped our hand, and he poured some rosewater in our hands, and we went in. And then after we were all in[side], he himself came in[side] and went and stood before the Shrine, and he chanted the Tablet of Visitation.

. . . perhaps the most memorable, the most affecting memory . . . for me [was] hearing the voice of Shoghi Effendi chant the Tablet of Visitation, because he had a heavenly, beautiful, melodious voice, and he had a way of chanting that was really unique. You never were conscious that he was doing anything to embellish or . . . to ornament the voice. All the emphasis was on the meaning of the words, and the raising and lowering [of] the dynamics of the chanting all brought out the inner meanings. And there are passages in that Tablet of Visitation that to this day, whether they are said in [the] original Arabic or . . . in [a] translation in English, I only hear his voice in my ears. . . . It was an unforgettable experience.

Then at the end of this he would come out, and some days he would just dismiss us, he would say good-bye, and he would return to the Master's house. Or on some days he would ask the attendants, the gardeners—and I remember the one who was in charge of the gardens around the Shrine; his name was Khosrow—he would say "Khosrow, bring some chairs and some tea from the pilgrim house," and the chairs would be set in the garden right in front of the Shrine, and we would be served tea. He would continue the discourse on that occasion until that time that he wanted to leave.[6]

Shoghi Effendi

Amín Banání's story of chanting a prayer for the Beloved Guardian (1934):

> I remember on one of the nights when I was there with my mother and other women from the East . . . I chanted [a prayer] in Persian, and after it was finished [Shoghi Effendi] said, "Now you must memorize one in Arabic." And so I of course immediately set to work to do that.[7]

Suheil Bu<u>sh</u>rú'í's story of first meeting the Beloved Guardian (1935):

> My earliest recollection of Shoghi Effendi dates back to when I was six or seven years old. I can never forget that afternoon when I accompanied my father on one of his many meetings with Shoghi Effendi. We arrived at the home of 'Abdu'l-Bahá, and we were ushered into the Guardian's reception room. As we entered the room, I noticed a figure that stood in the middle of the room and warmly greeted my father. It was a man—to me as a child that would seem—it was a man, but even as [a] child I realized that this was not a man like other men. There was an aura of majesty and sanctity about his person that filled me with awe. I watched the profound respect and intense reverence with which my father bowed to greet the majestic figure whose authority seemed to permeate everything around me.
>
> I asked, who is this man? With this question reeling through my young mind, I looked hard to see the face that I could not distinguish, for it was as though a flood of light had blinded my sight and I could see no more. That is the truth. Light seemed to emanate from his whole being. For me, as a child, this seemed a heavenly moment, and everything seemed to be

holy. . . . It seemed to me then, as it does now over many years later, that I was standing before God's ambassador on earth.

To this day I recapitulate those rare moments. I see how at the time, they could not be described except as mysterious, awe inspiring, and majestically glorious, for I was bereft of the profound spiritual significance that began to be associated with these early experiences as I became more and more aware of the Will and Testament of 'Abdu'l-Bahá.

Everyone who had the privilege and honor to visit Shoghi Effendi was struck by his solid presence and personality, his calm voice and courteous manner, his unmistakable compassion and unmitigated firmness not only in the principles and moral standards of the Faith. Everyone who visited him left his presence with an incredible impression of a rare and exceptional sanctity, whether the visit was a courtesy call or a business meeting.[8]

Suheil Bushrú'í's story of the Guardian's love of gardens (1935):

> . . . those of us in Haifa at the time knew that the Guardian loved gardens. . . . Shoghi Effendi loved nature, from the tiny rose to the lofty mountain. . . . Shoghi Effendi inherited from Bahá'u'lláh the love of beauty that celebrated balance and proportion in all things. . . .[9]

Suheil Bushrú'í's story of visiting the Shrines with the Beloved Guardian (1935):

> We followed Shoghi Effendi towards the Shrines whenever we went (zíyárat) visiting. . . . We used to meet at the pilgrim house. After the chanting of few prayers, Shoghi Effendi would

Shoghi Effendi

make a few statements on all matters related to world affairs, as well as the current affairs of the Faith. . . . Then we would all follow Shoghi Effendi to the Shrine of the Báb, which at the time was not yet completed . . . meaning the super-structure was not built. It was a custom of Shoghi Effendi to stand at the corner near the entrance of the Shrines of the Báb and 'Abdul-Bahá and anoint the believers with 'aṭṭár of roses as they passed to enter the Shrines. . . . 'Aṭṭár of roses—why? [It was] symbolic of the visit, that you meet your lord and master in the best apparel . . . so that one is absolutely sanctified, pure to stand before your creator. . . . I will always remember the small bottle of 'aṭṭár encased in an aluminum cover which the Guardian always took out of his pocket to anoint us, grown-ups and children alike, before entering the Holy Shrines. It was his way of following in the footsteps of 'Abdu'l-Bahá, Who considered Himself the Servant of the servants of God.

In every respect, it is that sense of holiness and purity that the Guardian wished the friends to develop in their relation-ships with the Central Figures of the Cause, and with the Cause itself. To wear the best apparel, to be clean and tidy in appearance, to be anointed with 'aṭṭár of roses, these helped elevate the soul and lift the spirit.

During these visits to the Shrines, the Guardian would en-ter last. The first visit would be to the sacred Tomb of the Báb, and the second to the sacred Tomb of 'Abdu'l-Bahá. One of the unforgettable experiences of anyone standing be-hind Shoghi Effendi is the way he chanted the two Tablets of Visitation. The one [is] in honor of the Báb, and the other is that marvelous Tablet of Visitation of 'Abdu'l-Bahá—in its Arabic style, inimitable. The spirit is a divine spirit. And there was something very special when the Guardian chanted that [Tablet]. He chanted it as though he was yearning, crying out for 'Abdu'l-Bahá. . . .

Of course he read the prayer—the Tablet of Visitation—not the way I read it, the Arabic way, but he did it the Persian way. But he instructed us, Arabic-speaking boys, to read in the Qur'ánic style. . . . One day in the pilgrim house he was talking about this, and he said "I asked the children to chant the prayers in the Arabic way, but I chant them in the Persian way," and he added, "'Abdu'l-Bahá told me to read the prayers in this way." The Guardian spoke perfect Arabic, perfect.[10]

Shoghi Effendi in the Gardens at Bahji

Iran Furútan Muhájir's story of following 'Amatu'l-Bahá Rúhíyyih <u>Kh</u>ánum to a special meeting (1941):

> . . . the ladies were taken to the sitting room in which 'Amatu'l-Bahá Rúhíyyih <u>Kh</u>ánum was awaiting us. 'Amatu'l-Bahá greeted us, bade us welcome and inquired about our trip. She spoke little Farsi, but we could understand her gentle phrases. It was only four years since her marriage to the Guardian, but

we could feel her serene majesty. Her radiance shone through her stunningly beautiful face.

. . . At the Master's House, as I was the only child among the pilgrims, I always sat close to 'Amatu'l-Bahá who sat on the mandar at the top of the room. One day we heard the beloved Guardian calling 'Amatu'l-Bahá. She jumped up and ran out of the room. I followed her. She opened the door to the private section of the House and went in and I followed. The Guardian was standing on top of the stairs. I looked up and he looked at me for a few seconds and talked to 'Amatu'l-Bahá. I was surprised that I did not understand what he was talking about. Of course the conversation was in English. He then went inside the apartment upstairs and 'Amatu'l-Bahá took my hand and the two of us returned to the sitting room. None of the lady pilgrims knew what had happened and I only told my parents about it when we returned to the Pilgrim House. They just kissed my eyes that had the bounty of gazing at the Guardian.[11]

Iran Furútan Muhájir's story of having a special seat next to the Beloved Guardian (1941):

When the Beloved Guardian returned from his walk with the men at the gardens of the Shrine, we were called to his presence. The ladies' meetings in his presence usually did not exceed thirty minutes. As was the custom with Persian women, we all sat quietly with bowed heads and listened to him without uttering a word, unless he asked a direct question of one of us. On the second day, when we entered the room, he bade me to go sit beside him. In our household the Guardian had such a lofty station that I was truly hesitant and shy to move. He smiled and again asked me to go to him. My mother nudged me forward and finally I went to sit on the sofa with him.

Those who have had the bounty of pilgrimage and have visited the room where the Guardian met the pilgrims know what an atmosphere it has. 'Abdu'l-Bahá used that room to greet his guests and he sat on the same sofa. A cushion covers His place and the Guardian sat at the other end of the sofa. As I had sat down a little further from him, the Guardian put his arm around my shoulders, pulled me to him and kept me there. He then told the ladies in the room, "She is the daughter of Jináb-i-Furútan." His blessings and bounties were showered upon me because of his affection for my father.

From that day onwards for the rest of the twenty-four days of our pilgrimage I sat close to the Guardian on the sofa.[12]

Iran Furútan Muhájir's story of chanting a prayer for the Beloved Guardian (1941):

One day he asked me to say a prayer. I stood up, folded my arms and chanted a short Persian prayer about servitude to the Blessed Perfection. The Guardian praised me to high heaven and again said, "She is the daughter of Jináb-i-Furútan." He then said, "the friends should teach their children Arabic, and Arabic prayers." From that day my father started teaching me to memorize an Arabic prayer. I still know it by heart and say it every day. On the last day of our pilgrimage when he was bidding us farewell, he caressed my head and my cheek and again repeated that I was Jináb-i-Furútan's daughter.[13]

Iran Furútan Muhájir's story of visiting the gardens of the Shrine of the Bab with the Beloved Guardian (1941):

> During our pilgrimage, on only one occasion did men and women have the bounty of being in the presence of the Guardian together outside the Pilgrim House. He led us all towards the Shrine and walked in the gardens. He offered rosebuds to all the pilgrims but did not enter the Shrine that day.[14]

Shoghi Effendi

The Greatest Holy Leaf

Stories with the Greatest Holy Leaf
Bahíyyih Khánum

Rúhu'lláh Varqá's story of teaching (1891):

> One day the Greatest Holy Leaf . . . asked [Rúhu'lláh] what they said to people when teaching the Faith.
>
> "We tell them," Rúhu'lláh answered, "that God has manifested Himself."
>
> Surprised at this remark, [the Greatest Holy Leaf] told them that surely they could not say such a thing straight away to people!
>
> "We don't tell this to everybody," responded Rúhu'lláh, "we only say it to those who have a capacity to hear such a statement."
>
> "How would you know such people?" asked [the Greatest Holy Leaf]. "We look into their eyes and then know whether we can give them the Message," replied Rúhu'lláh.
>
> [The Greatest Holy Leaf] laughed heartily and then beckoned Rúhu'lláh to come close to look into her eyes to find out whether she had the capacity for hearing such words. In obedience to her request, Rúhu'lláh sat down opposite the Greatest Holy Leaf, looked intently into her eyes and then said, "You already believe in these words."[1]

Rúḥá Aṣdaq's story of meeting the Greatest Holy Leaf (1913–14):

> At the entrance [of the House of the Master] stood the
> Greatest Holy Leaf who embraced my mother. . . . She then
> greeted each one of us and said, "I was unable to sleep all last
> night thinking what treatment the sea was giving to our visi-
> tors." Those beautiful eyes, that gaze, that gait, that dignity, I
> can never forget. We stayed in the house of 'Abdu'l-Bahá. . . .[2]

Rúḥá Aṣdaq's story of the Greatest Holy Leaf's love of music
(1913–14):

> One day she asked us, "Have you learned any new poems
> lately?" There was one poem recently popular in schools that
> was being taught as a nationalistic song. It referred to the loss
> of everything in the country, its wealth and its culture, and had
> a sad tune. When we finished she said, "I didn't ask for this.
> This was like a refrain for the dead!" Another time she said,
> "If one day you come across a fresh stream, gently trickling
> on clear sand, or hear a nightingale warble or hear a genuine
> kuchihbahi (a type of Persian folk song), think of me." Our
> hearts were crushed by the intensity of her longing.[3]

Rúḥá Aṣdaq's story of serving the Greatest Holy Leaf (1913–14):

> One day after lunch the Greatest Holy Leaf was resting on
> her bed and called me, "Rúḥá, come and rub my feet, they
> are very tired and painful." Willingly I entered the room and
> began gently rubbing her feet. She fell asleep. Some time later
> she suddenly looked at me and said, "You are still here?" She
> then pressed my hands in hers. My whole family had been out

looking for me, oblivious that I might be with the Greatest Holy Leaf all this time.[4]

The Greatest Holy Leaf

Rúḥá Aṣdaq's story of the approval of the Greatest Holy Leaf (1914):

> We the young sisters were exhilarated, joyous and witty. We
> were full of pleasure when we noted that we had at times made
> the Greatest Holy Leaf happy. One day she told our mother,
> "Ḍíyá'u'l-Ḥájíyyih, you did very well in bringing the young
> ones with you. Friends usually think of pilgrimage when they
> become old."[5]

Rúḥá Aṣdaq's story of her departure (1914):

> The appointed hour arrived. After breakfast 'Abdu'l-Bahá
> said, "Today prepare sweet food for our travelers." The Greatest
> Holy Leaf said, "Sweet enough so as to forget the bitterness of
> separation." He replied, "No sweetness can compensate for the
> bitterness of separation."
>
> After lunch began the anguish of farewell, beginning with
> 'Abdu'l-Bahá. I don't even remember what transpired other
> than that we were parting from the Motive of our existence.
> We then found ourselves in the kind arms of the Greatest Holy
> Leaf and bade farewell to her. With much difficulty we left the
> other friends. Watching the sadness on my parents' face made
> me forget my own grief. The Greatest Holy Leaf said, "I have
> never witnessed such a tearful farewell."
>
> As we watched with tearful eyes the house of the Master, we
> saw a servant rushing breathlessly towards us with a cup saying,
> "The Master has sent this rose-water for you to dip." This was
> to be the last kind gesture of our Lord.[6]

Bahíyyih Winckler's story of having tea with the Greatest Holy Leaf
(1919):

Mother and I were invited to have tea with the Master's family in the afternoon. Tea was served in the room opposite the front door of the Master's home. The Greatest Holy Leaf [and the women of the family] were there. They greeted us with love and were eager to hear news of America. The Master sat with us for a while. He read the newspapers, but He talked with us just the same.[7]

The Greatest Holy Leaf

Bahíyyih Winckler's story of learning to cook rice (1919):

> . . . the Greatest Holy Leaf told us that she would show us how to cook the rice we liked so much. We went to a little room where a charcoal fire was burning. The rice was washed and put into boiling salt water until it was just soft enough to break—about four or five minutes. It was then strained, and some butter was put in the pot and browned a little. The rice

was slowly added with a sprinkling of spices and some tiny pieces of meat. On top of this were placed two large pieces of butter, and the cover was replaced. This was put on a slow charcoal fire, and ashes and more charcoal were placed on top. It remained this way for three quarters of an hour.[8]

Bahíyyih Winckler's story of being with the Greatest Holy Leaf (1919):

> I walked around in the house because it was still raining outside. I saw a door standing partly open down a little hallway. It was the door to the room of the Greatest Holy Leaf. I was quiet, but the Greatest Holy Leaf heard me and asked me to come in. She was on her bed, and I was sorry to have disturbed her, but she smiled and got up to show me some interesting pictures and things that she had. She spoke little English, but her eyes talked. Her face looked dreadfully tired, but her eyes were like the Master's, so alive and expressive. She was not like the other ladies.
>
> The Greatest Holy Leaf was apart, like the Master. It was a joy to be with her. I loved her. She gave me a Persian pen box before I left. The pen box, which was decorated with birds and flowers, held bamboo pens and a small box of dry ink.
>
> Mother often sat beside the Greatest Holy Leaf in the afternoons because she, too, felt something special. A few days before we left, the Greatest Holy Leaf also gave us a piece of rock candy that Bahá'u'lláh used to give to those who visited Him in the Riḍván Garden. It was the last piece she had! It looked like crystal.[9]

'Alí Na<u>kh</u>javání's story of a delicious mouthful (1926):

About 1926 or 1927, when I was about five or six years old, I came to the Master's house with my mother one hot afternoon—it was probably during the summer months—and the door of the house was open. The Greatest Holy Leaf was seated next to the big round table which is still there in the hall of the Master's house. The samovar was next to her. . . . We reached the hall and stood there and bowed, I following my mother's example. <u>Kh</u>ánum looked at us and told us to come in. She was having tea. As I came closer I saw that she was having fresh Arabic bread, white cheese and fresh mint. These were placed on the table. She had made one mouthful of bread, cheese and mint, apparently intending to have it herself. It was ready to be eaten and she was still holding it in her hand. As we approached she asked me to come forward and I moved closer to her. She then asked me to close my eyes and I dutifully closed them. Then she said, "Open your mouth!" and she put the tidbit in my mouth. So vivid is this experience that every time I recall it I feel that I can taste that fresh mint, bread and cheese from the hand of the Greatest Holy Leaf. I feel and taste it every time I bring the incident to memory.[10]

'Alí Na<u>kh</u>javání's story of the gift of a shilling (1926):

My brother, Jalál, was two years older than I was. The second story is about him. I was not present on one occasion when he was leaving the presence of the Greatest Holy Leaf. It was at the time of the Mandate when we had British currency. She placed one shilling in his hand and said, "Jalál, here is a shilling, half for you and half for your brother." Jalál said, "But <u>Kh</u>ánum, how can I break this coin?" She laughed and beckoned him to her and gave him another shilling. "This one is for your brother."[11]

103

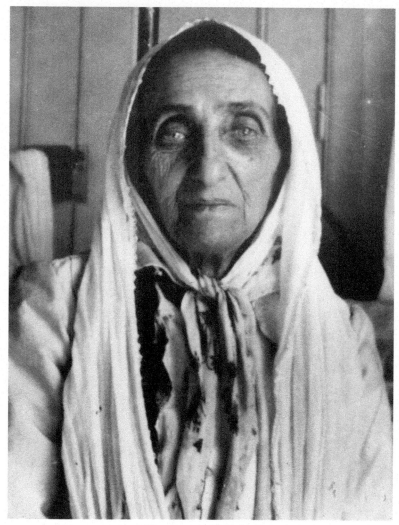

The Greatest Holy Leaf

'Alí Nakhjavání's story of the generosity of the Greatest Holy Leaf (1926):

> Many were the times my brother and I had sweetmeats, nuts, cookies and other goodies in her room. Often she was tired and would be seated or in bed. She would say, "Bring that box from under the mandar. Bring it out—that's right, bring it out. Now open it. Take one for yourself and give one to your brother."[12]

'Alí Nakhjavání's story of viewing the portraits of Bahá'u'lláh and the Báb (1926):

> How many times I have gone into that room in great reverence and knelt down, as we used to before the portraits of Bahá'u'lláh and the Báb, and watched there while the Greatest Holy Leaf sat there reverently unveiling the portraits and then closing them up again after the viewing was over.[13]

A picnic as observed by Marjory Morten (1931):

> So alive was [the Greatest Holy Leaf] to the source of all bounty that she had no consciousness of her own bounty. When she made a gift she seemed to be thanking you for it. The prompting included gratitude. When she gave joy she blessed you for it. It was almost as if she did not distinguish giving from receiving: as when, during the last year of her life, she went one summer day to the mountain with the children . . . and sat watching them at their picnic. To have her there with them made the day a festival. This joy that she shed she shared. . . . And when they came down in the evening she

thanked them for her delight in their play and for the happiness their happiness had given her.[14]

The Greatest Holy Leaf

Stories with the Holy Mother
Munírih <u>Kh</u>ánum

Munírih <u>Kh</u>ánum, the Holy Mother

Chanting with the women and children, as observed by Effie Baker:

> She loved to gather the women and children around her, and
> in her sweet voice chant with them the Holy Words and the
> poems written in praise of her Beloved One.[1]

Hand of the Cause of God Amatu'l-Bahá Rúḥíyyih Khánum, with her mother the Martyr and Disciple of 'Abdu'l-Bahá May Maxwell in Egypt in 1923

Stories about Hand of the Cause of God Amatu'l-Bahá Rúḥíyyih Khánum as a Child

A Tablet from the Master to her mother when she was seven months old (1911):

> In the garden of existence a rose hath bloomed with the utmost freshness, fragrance and beauty. Educate her according to the divine teachings so that she may grow up to be a real Bahá'í and strive with all thy heart, that she may receive the Holy Spirit.
>
> 'Abdu'l-Bahá[1]

Meeting the Beloved Guardian for the first time when she was twelve years old (1923):

> Rúḥíyyih Khánum often described her first encounter with the youthful Guardian. The day after their arrival in Haifa, she and her mother were in the old Pilgrim House opposite the home of 'Abdu'l-Bahá on Persian Street, where they were staying, when a visitor came to the door. Mrs. Maxwell, who had suffered from insomnia on the voyage over, was finally sleeping after several broken nights, and Mary [Rúḥíyyih

Khánum], in her concern for her mother, was determined that no one should disturb her. When the door opened a young man stepped into the hall and asked to see Mrs. Maxwell. Rúḥíyyih Khánum recounts: "I pulled myself up to my full height and said, 'Mrs. Maxwell is resting; who is it who wants to see her?'"

"I'm Shoghi Effendi," was the young man's bemused reply—at which young Mary gasped and fled into her mother's room. Quite forgetting her concern to allow May an uninterrupted sleep, she dived beneath the pillow, "like a puppy," as she always put it, and woke her up. When her mother asked her what on earth was the matter, Mary could only manage to say "He's here! He's here!" and, burrowing her head further into the pillows, point to the hall behind her. Upon realizing the situation, May said to her daughter, "Now Mary, pull yourself together and go and tell him I am coming."[2]

Dancing for the Greatest Holy Leaf (1923):

During her first pilgrimage, the Greatest Holy Leaf had asked to see Mary's performance of the Egyptian "shimmy," which she had learned that summer in Port Said, and had laughed till the tears rolled down her cheeks when young Mary, dressed in full costume, with kohl around her eyes and a drum under her arm, had sung and danced before her in the Master's House.[3]

A love of animals (1924):

. . . Mary arrived the following day [from Bahjí to Haifa] with a regular menagerie, including rats, cats, owls and chickens, so she had to leave a number of dogs in Bahjí. However you will be glad to know, she has developed beautifully and promises to combine the love and charm of her mother's with the freshness of youth.[4]

A letter to her mother about getting at least two extra kisses (1926):

Really I am having a fine time; I get at least two extra kisses from everyone just because I am your daughter and they are sending them back to you! Everyone loves you so much. Shoghi Effendi's first words were how you were and if you could walk and were well? And everyone else too, asks me first about you and your health. . . . Munírih Khánum just came here and she says for me to send you her love and tell you that every time she looks at me she wishes more that you were here! Everybody says I am the image of you when you first came to 'Akká and that they feel I am like you in every way this of course is the greatest compliment anyone can pay me![5]

Praying at the Shrine of 'Abdu'l-Bahá (1926):

You know, Mother, that it is not necessary or possible for me to write you what I felt in the tomb of the Master. I can only say that my first prayer was prayed as though you prayed it. I cried very hard when I first entered the Master's tomb, but after a little while I was filled with such joy and happiness that it was almost sacrilegious to be so full of joy when everyone else was crying. I cannot help it but the only thought I had was "how can we cheer our Guardian if we have nothing but tears and sighs, and why do we come to our Lord weeping with sorrow for His passing when He is not passed but here with us more so than ever."[6]

111

History of the Children

Badí' (1853–1870). Shoghi Effendi recounts the glorious story of Badí', the Martyr:

> Áqá Buzurg of <u>Kh</u>urásán, the illustrious "Badí'" (Wonderful); converted to the Faith by Nabíl; surnamed the "Pride of Martyrs"; the seventeen-year old bearer of the Tablet addressed to Násiri'd-Dín <u>Sh</u>áh; in whom, as affirmed by Bahá'u'lláh, "the spirit of might and power was breathed," was arrested, branded for three successive days, his head beaten to a pulp with the butt of a rifle, after which his body was thrown into a pit and earth and stones heaped upon it. After visiting Bahá'u'lláh in the barracks, during the second year of His confinement, he had arisen with amazing alacrity to carry that Tablet, alone and on foot, to Ṭihrán and deliver it into the hands of the sovereign. A four months' journey had taken him to that city, and, after passing three days in fasting and vigilance, he had met the <u>Sh</u>áh proceeding on a hunting expedition to <u>Sh</u>imírán. He had calmly and respectfully approached His Majesty, calling out, "O King! I have come to thee from Sheba with a weighty message"; whereupon at the Sovereign's order, the Tablet was taken from him and delivered to the mujtahids of Ṭihrán who were commanded to reply to that Epistle—a command which

they evaded, recommending instead that the messenger should be put to death. That Tablet was subsequently forwarded by the Sháh to the Persian Ambassador in Constantinople, in the hope that its perusal by the Sultán's ministers might serve to further inflame their animosity. For a space of three years Bahá'u'lláh continued to extol in His writings the heroism of that youth, characterizing the references made by Him to that sublime sacrifice as the "*salt of My Tablets.*"

He was in the presence of Bahá'u'lláh in 1869, and the stories included here are from when he was a youth of seventeen years.[1]

Zia Mabsoot Baghdádí (1882–1937). Dr. Zia Baghdádí was in the presence of Bahá'u'lláh in his childhood and would visit 'Abdu'l-Bahá in his youth. He had the privilege of being with 'Abdu'l-Bahá during His historic visits to North America, and he dug the first shovelful of earth at the ground-breaking ceremony of the Bahá'í House of Worship in Wilmette in 1921. The stories included here are from when he was a child of no more than ten years.[2]

Áqá Muḥammad-i-Tabrízí. The story from Áqá Muḥammad-i-Tabrízí is quoted by Hand of the Cause of God 'Alí Akbar Furútan in his book *Stories of Bahá'u'lláh*.

'Azízu'lláh Varqá (1881–1931). 'Azízu'lláh Varqá was the son of the Martyr, Hand of the Cause of God, and Apostle of Bahá'u'lláh 'Alí Muḥammad Varqá and the brother of Rúḥu'lláh Varqá the Martyr. He served on the first Bahá'í Local Spiritual Assembly of Ṭihrán. The stories included here are from his pilgrimage in 1891 when he was a child of ten years.[3]

Rúḥu'lláh Varqá (1883–1896). Rúḥu'lláh Varqá the Martyr was the son of the Martyr, Hand of the Cause of God, and Apostle of Bahá'u'lláh 'Alí-Muḥammad Varqá. He was martyred together with his father when he was only thirteen years old. A gifted poet, he had written a poem longing for his own martyrdom:

Welcome, O Cupbearer from the Ancient Feast!
Pour but a drop of Thy benevolence on this clay

that by Your bounty flecks of dust may become brilliant suns,
may become worthy of martyrdom before the Beloved.

O God, when will it take place that in Your quarter
I will sacrifice my life for my adoration of Your countenance?

How happy will be the day when in the field of love
I can surrender my life in the path of the Most Beloved of Lovers!

How joyous the moment when upon the gallows
I will brazenly proclaim the praises of the King of Bahá!

O God, when that day finally comes to pass,
I will at last become free from this withered body.

I will face towards the paradise of Eternity!
I will become verdant and fresh through the bounty of nearness!

The stories included here are taken from an account of his pilgrimage in 1891 when he was a child of eight years.[4]

Ṭarázu̇lláh Samandarí (1874–1968). Hand of the Cause of God Ṭarázu̇lláh Samandarí went on pilgrimage and attained the presence of Bahá'u'lláh in 1891. He was able to stay for six months in 'Akká, including one month after Bahá'u'lláh's passing in 1892. His extraordinary years of service spanned the last years of the ministry of Bahá'u'lláh, the ministry of 'Abdu'l-Bahá, the ministry of Shoghi Effendi, the period of stewardship of the Hands of the Cause, and the first five years of the Universal House of Justice. 'Abdu'l-Bahá described his upbringing in one of the Tablets revealed for him:

> . . . I supplicate before the Throne of Thy mercifulness and the threshold of Thy oneness that Thou mayest rain down Thy manifold confirmations and favours upon this servant of Thine who was born in the cradle of Thy love, nourished from the breast of Thy knowledge, reared in the lap of Thy servitude, nurtured in the bosom of Thy lifegiving Faith, until such time as he was fully developed through the outpourings of Thy bounty, attained maturity through Thy loving kindness and turned his face with devotion toward Thy countenance, with his heart wholly centered on Thee and his reliance completely placed in Thee . . .

The stories included here are from when Hand of the Cause of God Samandarí was a youth of seventeen years.[5]

Wendell Dodge (1883–1976). Wendell Dodge and his brother William were the sons of Arthur Dodge, a prominent American Bahá'í. The brothers went together on pilgrimage in 1901. By the time of 'Abdu'l-Bahá's visit to America in 1912, Wendell was a reporter for the New York City News Association, and he boarded the Cedric at quarantine and interviewed 'Abdu'l-Bahá. His article was given to all the New York newspapers, and, through the Associated Press, was sent to newspapers throughout the world. The stories included here are taken from Wendell's accounts that recall his experiences when he was a youth of eighteen years.[6]

William Dodge (1880–1973). William Dodge and his brother Wendell were the sons of Arthur Dodge, a prominent American Bahá'í. The brothers went together on pilgrimage in 1901. The stories included here are from when William was twenty-one years old.[7]

Mírzá Badí' Bushrú'í (1892–1973). Mírzá Badí' Bushrú'í lived in the Holy Land from 1902 to 1905, then attended the Syrian Protestant College, from which he would return to the Holy Land during breaks from school. When the British Government was awarded a mandate to govern Palestine in 1922, 'Abdu'l-Bahá put Mírzá Badí''s name forward to serve. He was accepted and went on to serve in Haifa, Tiberias, Nazareth, Nablus, and Jenin. In 1948, he moved to Egypt, where he served for many years as the chairman of the National Spiritual Assembly of Egypt and the Sudan. The stories included here are taken from his accounts in 1902 when he was a child of ten, and in 1914, when he was a youth of sixteen.[8]

Arna True (1890–1975). Arna True was the daughter of Hand of the Cause of God Corrine True. The stories included here are from her pilgrimage in 1907, when she was a youth of seventeen.[9]

Howard Kinney (1905–1938). Howard Kinney and his brother Sanford went on pilgrimage in 1909 with their parents. Referring to Howard and Sanford, 'Abdu'l-Bahá said to their parents, "They are My children, not yours." Howard had the privilege of being with 'Abdu'l-Bahá during His historic visit to North America in 1912.

The stories included here are from their pilgrimage in 1909, when he was a child of four years.[10]

Sanford Kinney (1900 to 1919). Sanford Kinney and his brother Howard went on pilgrimage in 1909 with their parents. The Kinney family had the privilege of hosting 'Abdu'l-Bahá for nine days during His historic visit to North America in 1912. The following prayer was revealed by 'Abdu'l-Bahá in Sanford's honor when he passed away:

For 'Abdu'l-'Alí Sanford Kinney—Upon him be Baha-el Abhá!

He is God!

O Thou divine Providence!

Sanford was a child of the Kingdom and, like unto a tender shrub, was in the utmost freshness and grace in the Abhá Paradise. He has ascended to the world of the Kingdom, that in the ev-er-lasting rose-garden he may grow and thrive on the banks of the river of Everlasting Life and may blossom and attain fruition.

O Thou divine Providence! Rear him by the outpouring of the cloud of mercy and nourish him through the heat of the sun of pardon and of forgiveness. Stir him by the breeze of bounty and bestow patience and forbearance upon his kind father and mother, that they may not deplore his separation, and may rest assured in meeting their son in the everlasting kingdom. Thou art the Forgiving and the Compassionate!

'Abdu'l-Bahá Abbas
(Haifa, Palestine, November 23, 1919.)[11]

The stories included here are from the pilgrimage in 1909, when he was a child of nine years.

Rúḥá Aṣdaq Khodadost (1898–1982). Rúḥá Aṣdaq Khodadost was the daughter of Hand of the Cause of God Ibn-i-Aṣdaq and Ḍíyá'u'l-Ḥájíyyih, and the granddaughter of Hand of the Cause of God Ismu'lláhu'l-Aṣdaq. She lived in Iran for many years, homefront pioneering in Riḍ'íyyih where she served with other pioneers such as the Hand of the Cause of God Rahmatu'llah Muhajir. She later moved to Denmark as a pioneer. She received the following Tablet from 'Abdu'l-Bahá in her youth:

He is the All-Glorious!

For the attention of the blessed leaf, Ruha, upon her be the Glory of God, the All-Glorious!

He is the All-Glorious!

O thou illumined leaf!

A hundred thousand maidservants, who for countless years engaged in divers arduous devotions, and who, with fervent longing and tearful lamentation, supplicated the threshold of Divine Oneness that they might live for but a moment in these Days and perceive the merest glimmer of the Sinaitic fire, expired at last in the wilderness of separation, and, with infinite regret, laid down their lives in love's arena. Thou, however, having neither expended effort, nor suffered hardship, nor experienced the fatigue of arduous devotions, hast, through purest grace and bounty, become a recipient of this bestowal from

Him Who is the Lord of the seen and the unseen, attained unto the Days of God, and been favoured with a boundless outpouring of His mercy and loving-kindness.

Upon thee be the Glory of God!

'Abdu'l-Bahá

The stories included here are from her pilgrimage in 1914, when she was a youth of sixteen years.[12]

'Alí Yazdí (1899–1978). 'Alí Yazdí first met 'Abdu'l-Bahá as a child in Ramlah. The stories included here are from his visits to the Holy Land in 1917, as a youth of eighteen years.[13]

Bahíyyih Randall Winckler (1907–2000). Bahíyyih Randall Winckler met 'Abdu'l-Bahá for the first time in 1912 during His historic visit to North America, then went on pilgrimage in 1919. During her pilgrimage, 'Abdu'l-Bahá gave her the name Bahíyyih. She pioneered to South Africa in 1953 at the direction of Shoghi Effendi and served there on the National Spiritual Assembly as well as on the Continental Board of Counselors. The stories included here are from her pilgrimage in 1919, with her parents William Henry Randall and Ruth Randall, when she was a child of twelve years.[14]

'Azíz Ismayn Yazdí (1909–2004). 'Azíz Ismayn Yazdí moved with his family to the Holy Land in 1919, where they stayed for three years until 1921. After many years of pioneering and service to the Cause, he was appointed to the first International Teaching Center in 1973, where he served for fifteen years. The stories included here are from his stay in the Holy Land, when he was a child of ten to twelve years.[15]

Sylvia Paine Parmalee (1909–2001). Sylvia Paine Parmalee was an active member of the Bahá'í community of the United States throughout her life. The stories included here are from her pilgrimage with her mother Mabel Hyde Paine in 1920, when she was a child of eleven years.[16]

'Alí Nakhjavání (1919–2019). 'Alí Nakhjavání spent his childhood in the Holy Land from the time he was two years old until he attended the American University of Beirut. After his distinguished services in Iran and Uganda, he moved back to the Holy Land when he was elected to the International Bahá'í Council. He was elected to the Universal House of Justice during its inaugural convention in 1963 and served as a member for forty years. The stories included here are from the time he was a child of seven years.[17]

Amín Banání (1927–2013). Professor Amín Banání was a Knight of Bahá'u'lláh for Greece, a member of the Board of Trustees of Ḥuqúqu'lláh for the United States for over two decades, and an advocate for the Faith at the United Nations. He was also a Professor of Persian History and Literature at the University of California, Los Angeles. The stories included here are from the time he was child of seven and a half years.[18]

Suheil Bushrú'í (1929–2015). Professor Suheil Bushrú'í was a distinguished scholar, academic, author, poet, critic, translator, and advocate for peace. He was born in the Holy Land and lived there during his childhood. He was the first person to hold the position of Bahá'í Chair for World Peace at the University of Maryland, and he held several other significant academic posts. The stories included here are from the time he was a child of six years.[19]

Iran Furútan Muhájir (1933–). Knight of Bahá'u'lláh to the Mentawai Islands Iran Furútan Muhájir has lived a life of pioneering and service to the Cause from her earliest childhood. She is a distinguished author and has kindly shared the stories included here from her pilgrimage with her father Hand of the Cause of God 'Alí Akbar Furútan and her mother 'Aṭá'íyyih Furútan in 1941 when she was a child of seven years.[20]

Notes

Stories with the Blessed Beauty Bahá'u'lláh

1. The dates in parentheses refer to the dates the story took place.
2. Myron Phelps, *The Master in 'Akká,* pp. 80–81.
3. Jináb-i-Faḍíl, "The Glory of Deeds," *Star of the West,* vol. 14, no. 6 (September, 1923): 174.
4. Baharieh Ma'ání, *Leaves of the Twin Divine Trees,* p. 322.
5. *The Bahá'í World,* vol. VII, pp. 539.
6. 'Alí Akbar Furútan, *Stories of Bahá'u'lláh,* pp. 69–70.
7. The Martyr, Hand of the Cause of God and Apostle of Bahá'u'lláh Mírzá 'Alí-Muḥammad Varqá.
8. As told by Martha Root in *Star of the West,* vol. 23, no. 3 (June, 1932): 72–73.
9. Ibid., pp. 73–74.
10. The Martyr, Hand of the Cause of God and Apostle of Bahá'u'lláh Mírzá 'Alí-Muḥammad Varqá.
11. 'Alí Akbar Furútan, *Stories of Bahá'u'lláh,* p. 71.
12. Kiser Barnes, *Stories of Bahá'u'lláh and Some Notable Believers,* pp. 173–74.
13. Ṭarázu'lláh Samandarí, *Moments with Bahá'u'lláh: Memoirs of the Hand of the Cause of God Ṭarázu'lláh Samandarí,* p. 43.
14. Ibid., pp. 43–48.

15. Ibid., pp. 51–55
16. Ibid., pp. 55–57.
17. Ibid., pp. 66–67.
18. Ibid., p. 69.
19. Ibid., pp. 22–23.
20. Ibid., pp. 40–41.
21. Ibid., pp. 8–11.
22. Ibid., pp. 17–20.

Stories with the Beloved Master 'Abdu'l-Bahá

1. Marzieh Gail, *Summon Up Remembrance,* p. 235.
2. Ibid., p. 138.
3. William Dodge, "My Visits with 'Abdu'l-Baha in 1901 & 1912—transcript of a recording by William Copeland Dodge," February 6th, 1959, http://bahaitalks.blogspot.com/2013/08/my-visits-with-abdul-bha-in-1901-1912.html.
4. Ibid.
5. Ibid.
6. Ibid.
7. Ibid.
8. Mona Khademi, *Heavenly Attributes: The Character of 'Abdu'l-Bahá Seen Through the Eyes of Easterners and Two Westerners,* p. 11.
9. Ibid.
10. Dr. Youness Afroukteh, *Memories of Nine Years in 'Akká,* pp. 159–60.
11. Ibid., pp. 204–6.
12. Lady Blomfield, *The Chosen Highway,* pp. 230–31.
13. Mary Lucas, "A Brief Account of My Visit to Acca," p. 5, http://bahai-library.com/lucas_my_visit_acca.

14. Nathan Rutstein, *Corinne True: Faithful Handmaid of 'Abdu'l-Bahá,* pp. 57–59.

15. Ibid., p. 65.

16. Juliet Thompson, *The Diary of Juliet Thompson,* p. 68.

17. Ibid., pp. 40–41.

18. Ibid., pp. 43–44.

19. *Star of the West,* vol. 9, no. 3 (April 28, 1918): 36.

20. Ibid., no. 11 (September 27, 1918): 121–22.

21. Ibid., vol. 5, no. 5 (June 5, 1914): 74.

22. Rúhá Aşdaq, *One Life One Memory,* pp. 24–26.

23. Ibid., pp. 27–28.

24. Ibid., p. 30.

25. Ibid., p. 31.

26. Ibid., pp. 31–32.

27. Ibid., p. 32.

28. Ibid.

29. Lady Blomfield, *The Chosen Highway,* pp. 211–12.

30. Ibid., p. 216.

31. Marzieh Gail, <u>*Khánum: The Greatest Holy Leaf,*</u> p. 26.

32. 'Alí M. Yazdí, *Blessings Beyond Measure: Recollections of 'Abdu'l-Bahá and Shoghi Effendi,* pp. 25–27.

33. Ibid., pp. 27–28.

34. Ibid., p. 33.

35. Ibid.

36. Bahíyyih Winckler, *My Pilgrimage to Haifa November 1919,* pp. 4–9.

37. Ibid., pp. 10–13.

38. Ibid., pp. 14–15.

39. Ibid., pp. 16–17.

40. Ibid., p. 20.

41. Ibid., pp. 27–28.

42. Ibid., pp. 28–29.

43. Ibid., pp. 20–23.

44. Ibid., p. 87.

45. Ibid., p. 29.

46. Ibid., p. 89.

47. Ibid., p. 29.

48. Ibid., pp. 35–36.

49. Ibid., pp. 38–41.

50. Ibid., pp. 81–85.

51. Azíz Yazdí, "Remembrances of 'Abdu'l-Bahá by Aziz Yazdi," https://www.youtube.com/watch?v=hkyXFJf.

52. Ibid.

53. Ibid.

54. Ibid.

55. Azíz Yazdí, "Bahá'í World Congress 1992—Stories with Master," https://www.youtube.com/watch?v=4pLKq9TL660.

56. *Star of the West*, vol. 12, no. 12 (October 16, 1921): 196–197.

57. Ibid., no. 13 (November 4, 1921): 213–14.

58. Sylvia Paine, "Bahá'í World Congress 1992—Stories with Master," https://www.youtube.com/watch?v=4pLKq9TL660.

Stories about Shoghi Effendi as a Child

1. Rúḥíyyih Rabbání, *The Priceless Pearl*, p. 5.

2. Riaz Khadem, *Prelude to the Guardianship*, pp. 3–4.

3. Dr. Youness Afroukteh, *Memories of Nine Years in 'Akká*, pp. 59–60.

4. Rúḥíyyih Rabbání, *The Priceless Pearl*, p. 9.

5. Ibid., p. 10.

6. *The Bahá'í World*, vol. XVIII, p. 60.

7. Rúḥíyyih Rabbání, *The Priceless Pearl*, pp. 8.

8. Kathryn Hogenson, *Lighting the Western Sky: The Hearst Pilgrimage and the Establishment of the Bahá'í Faith in the West*, pp. 111–12.

9. Marzieh Gail, *Summon Up Remembrance*, pp. 258–59.

10. Rúḥíyyih Rabbání, *The Priceless Pearl*, pp. 7–8.

11. Ibid., pp. 8–9.

12. Ibid., p. 9.

13. A. Q. Faizi, *Stories from the Delight of Hearts*, p. 162.

14. Rúḥíyyih Rabbání, *The Priceless Pearl*, p. 10.

15. Ibid., p. 15.

16. Ugo Giachery, *Shoghi Effendi, Recollections*, pp. 14–15.

17. *The Bahá'í World*, vol. IV, p. 396.

18. Marzieh Gail, *Summon Up Remembrance*, p. 284.

19. Rúḥíyyih Rabbání, *The Priceless Pearl*, pp. 15–16.

20. Jan Jasion, *Never Be Afraid to Dare: The Story of 'General Jack,'* pp. 31–32.

21. Marzieh Gail, <u>*Khánum: The Greatest Holy Leaf*,</u> pp. 30–31.

22. Riaz Khadem, *Prelude to the Guardianship*, p. 4.

23. Rúḥá Aṣdaq, *One Life One Memory*, p. 33.

24. Ugo Giachery, *Shoghi Effendi, Recollections*, p. 119.

Stories with the Beloved Guardian Shoghi Effendi

1. Mona Khademi, *Heavenly Attributes: The Character of 'Abdu'l-Baha Seen Through the Eyes of Easterners and Two Westerners*, p. 11.

2. Bahíyyih Winckler, *My Pilgrimage to Haifa November 1919*, pp. 37–38.

3. Ibid., pp. 65–69.

4. Ibid., pp. 75–76.

5. 'Alí Nakhjavání, in *The Bahá'í World,* vol. XVIII, pp. 63–64.

6. Amín Banání, *The World Order of Bahá'u'lláh (Talk 1 of 3)—A Talk by Professor Amín Banání,* https://www.youtube.com/watch?v=sjD-OR178ro.

7. Ibid.

8. Suheil Bushrú'í, "Bahá'í World Congress 1992—Stories with Master," https://www.youtube.com/watch?v=4pLKq9TL660.

9. Ibid.

10. Ibid.

11. Iran Furútan Muhájir, personal recollections.

12. Ibid.

13. Ibid.

14. Ibid.

Stories with the Greatest Holy Leaf Bahíyyih Khánum

1. Kiser Barnes, *Stories of Bahá'u'lláh and Some Notable Believers,* p. 174.

2. Rúhá Aṣdaq, *One Life One Memory,* p. 23.

3. Ibid., p. 34.

4. Ibid., p. 35.

5. Ibid., pp. 37–38.

6. Ibid., p. 41.

7. Bahíyyih Winckler, *My Pilgrimage to Haifa November 1919,* p. 25.

8. Ibid., p. 92.

9. Ibid., pp. 43–49.

10. 'Alí Nakhjavání, in *The Bahá'í World,* vol. XVIII, p. 63.

11. Ibid.

12. Ibid.

13. Ibid.

14. Marjory Morten, in *The Bahá'í World,* vol. V, p. 182.

Stories with the Holy Mother Munírih <u>Kh</u>ánum

1. *The Bahá'í World.* vol. VIII, p. 267.

Stories about Hand of the Cause of God
Amatu'l-Bahá Rúḥíyyih <u>Kh</u>ánum as a Child

1. Violette Na<u>kh</u>javání, *A Tribute to Amatu'l-Bahá Rúḥíyyih <u>Kh</u>ánum*, p. 3.
2. Violette Na<u>kh</u>javání, *The Maxwells of Montreal: Vol. 2: Middle Years 1923–1937, Late Years 1937–1952*, p. 5.
3. Violette Na<u>kh</u>javání, *A Tribute to Amatu'l-Bahá Rúḥíyyih <u>Kh</u>ánum*, p. 14.
4. From a letter by Siegfried Schopflocher to Rúḥíyyih <u>Kh</u>ánum's father, William Sutherland Maxwell, in Violette Na<u>kh</u>javání, *The Maxwells of Montreal: Vol. 2: Middle Years 1923–1937, Late Years 1937–1952*, p. 17.
5. From a letter from Rúḥíyyih <u>Kh</u>ánum to her mother May Maxwell, in Violette Na<u>kh</u>javání, *The Maxwells of Montreal: Vol. 2: Middle Years 1923–1937, Late Years 1937–1952*, pp. 66–67.
6. From a letter from Rúḥíyyih <u>Kh</u>ánum to her mother May Maxell, in Violette Na<u>kh</u>javání, *The Maxwells of Montreal: Vol. 2: Middle Years 1923–1937, Late Years 1937–1952*, pp. 66–67.

History of the Children

1. Shoghi Effendi, *God Passes By*, pp. 314–15.
2. *The Bahá'í World*, vol. VII, pp. 536–39.
3. H. M. Balyuzi, *Eminent Bahá'ís in the time of Bahá'u'lláh*, p. 80.
4. John Hatcher and Amrollah Hemmat, *Reunion with the Beloved: Poetry and Martyrdom*, pp. 69–72.
5. *The Bahá'í World*, vol. XV, pp. 410–15.
6. *Star of the West*, vol. III, no. 3 (April 28, 1912): 3.
7. Dodge, William Copeland. n.d. "My Visits with 'Abdu'l-Bahá in

1901 and 1912." http://bahaitalks.blogspot.com/2013/08/my-visits-with-abdul-bha-in-1901-1912.html. Accessed December 20, 2015.

8. *The Bahá'í World,* vol. XV, pp. 546–47.

9. Nathan Rutstein, *Corinne True: Faithful Handmaid of 'Abdu'l-Bahá,* p. 53.

10. *The Bahá'í World,* vol. VIII, p. 670.

11. *Star of the West,* vol. 10, no. 19 (March 2, 1920): 350.

12. Rúhá Aṣdaq, *One Life One Memory,* pp. 1–5.

13. 'Alí Yazdí, *Memories of 'Abdu'l-Bahá.* Accessed April 29, 2021. https://www.bahai.org/documents/essays/yazdi-ali-m/memories-abdul-baha.

14. *The Bahá'í World,* vol. XXIX, pp. 274–75.

15. Bahá'í World News Service. "Youthful experience inspired service," April 19, 2004. Accessed July 1, 2021. https://news.bahai.org/story/297/.

16. *Star of the West,* vol. 12, no. 10 (September 8, 1921): 163.

17. Bahá'í World News Service. "Two members of Universal House of Justice leave after 40 years service," April 29, 2003. Accessed July 1, 2021. https://news.bahai.org/story/206/.

18. National Spiritual Assembly of the Bahá'ís of the United States, "Amin Banani was an influential scholar and a Knight of Bahá'u'lláh," September-October, 2013. Accessed June 3, 2021. https://www.bahai.us/9/community/news/2013/september-october/amin-banani-was-an-influential-scholar-and-a-knight-of-bahaullah/.

19. University of Maryland College of Behavioral and Social Sciences. "Honoring the Life and Legacy of Professor Suheil Bushrui," n.d. Accessed April 29, 2021. https://bsos.umd.edu/featured-content/honoring-life-and-legacy.

20. Iran Furútan Muhájir, *Personal Recollections.*

Bibliography

Works of Shoghi Effendi

God Passes By. Wilmette, IL: Bahá'í Publishing Trust, 2010.

Other Works

Afroukhteh, Dr. Youness. *Memories of Nine Years in 'Akká.* Oxford: George Ronald, 2005.

Aṣdaq, Rúhá. *One Life One Memory.* Oxford: George Ronald, 1999.

Bahá'í Perspective. "Bahá'í World Congress 1992—Stories with Master." Accessed June 4, 2021. https://www.youtube.com/watch?v=4pLKq9TL660.

Bahá'í World News Service. "Two members of Universal House of Justice leave after 40 years service." April 29, 2003. Accessed April 29, 2021. https://news.bahai.org/story/206/.

———. "Youthful experience inspired service." April 19, 2004. Accessed July 1, 2021. https://news.bahai.org/story/297/.

Balyuzi, H. M. *Eminent Bahá'ís in the time of Bahá'u'lláh.* Oxford. George Ronald. 1985.

Banani, Amin. "The World Order of Bahá'u'lláh, A Talk by Professor Amin Banani, Talk 1 of 3, Santa Monica, California." 2003. Accessed June 3, 2021. https://www.youtube.com/watch?v=s-jD-OR178ro.

Barnes, Kiser. *Stories of Bahá'u'lláh and Some Notable Believers.* New Delhi: Bahá'í Publishing Trust, 2003.

Blomfield, Lady. *The Chosen Highway.* King's Lynn: George Ronald, 2007.

Bushrú'í, Dr. Suheil. "Memories of Shoghi Effendi." Talk given at the Persian Arts and Letters Conference, 2012.

Dodge, William Copeland. "My Visits with 'Abdu'l-Bahá in 1901 and 1912." N.d. Accessed December 20, 2015. http://bahaitalks.blogspot.com/2013/08/my-visits-with-abdul-bha-in-1901-1912.html.

Faizi, A. Q. *Stories from the Delight of Hearts.* Los Angeles: Kalimat Press, 1980.

Furútan, 'Alí Akbar. *Stories of Bahá'u'lláh.* Oxford: George Ronald, 1986.

Gail, Marzieh. *Khánum: The Greatest Holy Leaf.* Oxford: George Ronald, 1982.

———. *Summon Up Remembrance.* Oxford: George Ronald, 1987.

Giachery, Ugo. *Shoghi Effendi, Recollections.* Oxford: George Ronald, 1973.

Hatcher, John S., and Amrollah Hemmat. *Reunion with the Beloved: Poetry and Martyrdom.* Hong Kong: Juxta Publishing Limited, 2004.

Hogenson, Kathryn Jewett. *Lighting the Western Sky: The Hearst Pilgrimage and the Establishment of the Bahá'í Faith in the West.* Oxford: George Ronald, 2010.

Jasion, Jan Teofil. *Never Be Afraid to Dare: The Story of 'General Jack.'* Oxford: George Ronald, 2001.

Khadem, Riaz. *Prelude to the Guardianship.* Oxford: George Ronald, 2014.

Khademi, Mona. *Heavenly Attributes: The Character of 'Abdu'l-Bahá Seen Through the Eyes of Easterners and Two Westerners.* Los Angeles: Ketab Corp, 2012.

Lucas, Mary. "A Brief Account of My Visit to Acca." *Bahá'í Library Online*. 1905. Accessed December 21, 2015. http://bahai-library.com/lucas_my_visit_acca.

Ma'ani, Baharieh Rouhani. *Leaves of the Twin Divine Trees*. Oxford: George Ronald, 2008.

Muhájir, Iran Furútan. "Personal Recollections." Unpublished manuscript. 2021.

Nakhjavání, Violette. *A Tribute to Amatu'l-Bahá Rúḥíyyih Khánum*. Thornhill: Bahá'í Canada Publication, 2000.

———. *The Maxwells of Montreal: Vol. 2: Middle Years 1923–1937; Late Years 1937–1952*. Oxford: George Ronald, 2012.

National Spiritual Assembly of the Bahá'ís of the United States. "Amin Banani was an influential scholar and a Knight of Bahá'u'lláh." September–October, 2013. Accessed June 3, 2021. https://www.bahai.us/9/community/news/2013/september-october/amin-banani-was-an-influential-scholar-and-a-knight-of-bahaullah/.

Phelps, Myron H. *The Master in 'Akká*. Los Angeles: Kalimat Press, 1985.

Rabbani, *Rúḥíyyih. The Priceless Pearl*. London: Bahá'í Publishing Trust, 1969.

Rutstein, Nathan. *Corinne True: Faithful Handmaid of 'Abdu'l-Bahá*. Oxford: George Ronald, 1987.

Samandarí, Ṭarázu'lláh. *Moments with Bahá'u'lláh: Memoirs of the Hand of the Cause of God Ṭarázu'lláh Samandarí*. Translated by Mehdi Samandarí and Marzieh Gail. Los Angeles: Kalimat Press, 1995.

Star of the West. Volumes 3, 5, 9, 12, 14, 23. Oxford: George Ronald, 1984.

The Bahá'í World. Volumes IV, V, VII, VIII, XV, XVIII, XXIX. Wilmette: Bahá'í Publishing Trust, 1981.

Thompson, Juliet. *The Diary of Juliet Thompson*. Los Angeles: Kalimat Press, 1983.

University of Maryland College of Behavioral and Social Sciences. *Honoring the Life and Legacy of Professor Suheil Bushrui*. N.d. Accessed April 29, 2021. https://bsos.umd.edu/featured-content/honoring-life-and-legacy.

Winckler, Bahíyyih Randall. *My Pilgrimage to Haifa November 1919*. Wilmette: Bahá'í Publishing Trust, 1996.

Yazdí, 'Alí M. *Blessings Beyond Measure: Recollections of 'Abdu'l-Bahá and Shoghi Effendi*. Wilmette: Bahá'í Publishing Trust, 1988.

———. *Memories of 'Abdu'l-Bahá*. N.d. Accessed April 29, 2021. https://www.bahai.org/documents/essays/yazdi-ali-m/memories-abdul-baha.

Yazdí, Azíz. *Remembrances of 'Abdu'l-Bahá by Azíz Yazdí*. December 15, 2019. Accessed June 4, 2021. https://www.youtube.com/watch?v=hkyXFJfD5y8.

Index

'Abdu'l-Bahá, 1, 3, 14–16, 19–58, 60–72, 74–77, 100, 101, 109

Afroukhteh, Dr. Youness, 23, 25

'Akká, locations in

    Abbúd, House of, 19

    'Abdu'lláh Páshá, House of, 19–23, 25–31, 60–68, 72–75, 79–80

    Bahjí, 110–11

        Mansion of, 4–13, 15–17, 39

        Pilgrim House at, 54, 69

        tent at, 13

    Caravanserai, 8, 15, 23–25, 28, *see* Khán, the

    Gate, the 14

    Junaynih, Garden of, 3, 9, 10

    Khán, the, 28

    mosque, 14

    Prison, the, 1–3, 12, 24, 25, 80, 113

    Riḍván, Garden of, 11–12, 80–82

    Shrine of Bahá'u'lláh, 51, 54–56, 70, 79–80, 82

'Amatu'l-Bahá Rúḥíyyih Khánum, vii, 109–11

'Andalíb, 9, 12

animals
  bees, 33
  birds, 33
  cats, 110
  chickens, 110
  dogs, 110
  donkey, 71, 81
  nightingale, 98
  owls, 110
  parrot, 62
  rats, 110
Arabic, 24, 30, 36, 87, 88, 91, 92, 94
Asadu'lláh, Mírzá, 72
Aṣdaq, Rúḥá, 34–39, 98–100, 119–20
Aṣdaq, Rúḥu'lláh, 38
Aṣdaq, Ṭáli'a, 36

Badí', 2–3, 113–14
Baghdádí, Zia Mabsoot, 4, 114
Bahá'u'lláh, 1–17
Baker, Effie, 107
Banání, Amín, 85, 88, 121
Bashir, 35–36
Beirut Syrian Protestant College, 32, 75
burial, 13
Bushrú'í, Mírzá Badí', 22–23, 33, 79, 117
Bushrú'í, Suheil, xv, 88–89, 121

celebrations
  Christian, 28
  Muslim, 28

Naw-Rúz, 8, 9

Nineteen Day Feast, 53

Riḍván, 11–12

sultan's coronation, anniversary of, 28

chanting, 4, 7, 10, 14, 20, 22, 28, 29, 36, 40, 41, 42, 46, 51, 52, 56, 61, 62, 65, 67, 68, 70, 82, 85, 86, 88, 89, 91, 92, 94, 107

contentment, 12

cooking, 9, 38, 101

courtesy, 67

Covenant, 16

dancing, 110

death of a child, 19, 40

Ḍíyá'u'l-Ḥájíyyih, 100, 119

Dodge, Arthur, 22, 116, 117

Dodge, Wendell, 20–22, 116

Dodge, William, 20–22, 117

dreams, 22, 61, 71–72

Effendi, Ḥusayn 3, 19

English, speaking in, 47

Esslemont, Dr. John, 48

Farsi, 92

Fujita, 47, 49, 50

Furútan, 'Alí Akbar, 93, 94, 114, 122

Furútan, 'Aṭá'iyyih, vii, 93, 94, 122

games, 30

gardens, 41, 54, 80, 81, 82, 87, 89, 95

generosity, 25

gifts,
    apple, 54
    baklava, 14
    cakes, 28, 39
    candy, 5, 57, 102
    clothing, 8, 40
    coins, 26, 103
    cookies, 105
    dates, 12, 49–50
    fruit, 28
    hyacinths, 29
    jasmine, 49
    money, 26, 54
    "mouthful of Khánum," 69, 103
    nuts, 105
    oranges, 12, 13–14
    Persian pen box, 102
    pomegranates, 80
    refreshments, 53
    ringstones, 22
    rock candy, 102
    rosebuds, 95
    roses, 10, 29, 40
    sharbat, 28
    shawl, 32
    sweet food, 100
    sweetmeats, 12, 105
    sweets, 5, 28, 38, 39
    tangerines, 30, 37
    tea, 31–32, 36, 38, 39
    tickets, 40

good conduct, 19–20, 26, 32–33

Goodall, Ella, 62–63

grapefruit, 80

Greatest Holy Leaf, 1, 23, 34, 36, 38, 48, 61, 62, 63, 65, 69, 72,
74–77, 83–85, 97–106, 110

Haifa, locations in
    Master, The House of, 32–44, 46–48, 50, 54, 71, 75–77, 80,
        82–84, 86–90, 92–94, 98–99, 100–3, 105, 110
    monastery school, 73–74
    Mount Carmel, 33, 43, 51, 65, 70–71, 86, 105–6
    Number 4 Haparsim Street, 44, 45, 48–50, 56, 109–10
    Pilgrim House, vii, 42, 85, 86, 87, 89, 92, 93, 95
    Shrine of 'Abdu'l-Bahá, 51, 53–54, 86, 91, 111
    Shrine of the Báb, 32, 42–43, 46, 50–52, 70, 82, 85–87,
        89–91, 93, 95

Ḥakím, Dr. Luṭfulláh, vii, 47, 48

Ḥaydar 'Alí, Haji Mírzá, 68

humor, xv, 21, 26, 41

Ibn-i-Aṣdaq, 119

Ismá'íl Áqá, 36–37

Káshání, Haji Ghulám-'Alí, 9

Khátún, Hájar, 71

Khosrow, 87

Kinney, Carrie, 31

Kinney, Howard, 30–32, 117

Kinney, Sanford, 31–32, 118

Latimer, George, 47

Lucas, Mary, 28–29

Maxwell, May, 109–11
meals, 9, 13, 20–22, 30, 38, 43, 83
   ábgús̱ht (Persian Stew), 38
   bread, 9, 36, 62, 103
   bread and sugar, 1
   cheese, 36, 62, 103
   chicken, 49
   chopsticks, 49
   dates, 49–50, 80
   halim (a porridge), 13
   lamb, 9
   lemons, 80
   macaroni, 30–31
   mint, 103
   olives, 36
   oranges, 14, 37
   picnic, 105
   pomegranates, 80
   potato, 49
   refreshments, 53
   rice, 43, 47, 49, 101–2
   shredded wheat, 49
   sweet coffee, 27
   sweet food, 100
   tea, 28, 31, 36, 87, 101
   tea and sweets, 38, 39
   watermelon, 80
   yogurt, 49–50

Mishkín-Qalam, 23, 24
morning prayers, 36, 62
Morten, Marjory, 105
Muhájir, Dr. Raḥmatu'lláh, xi, 119
Muhájir, Iran Furútan, vii, xi, 92–95, 122
Munírih Khánum, 65, 107, 111
music, 98
Mustafa, 3

Nabíl-i-Aʻẓam, 9
Nakhjavání, ʻAlí, vii, 82–84, 102–3, 105, 121
Nakhjavání, Jalál 82–84, 103, 105
new name,
    Badíʻa, 56–58
    Bahíyyih, 48
    Mabsoot, 4
Núri'd-Dín, Áqá Mírzá, 23–24

odes, *see* poetry

Paine, Mabel, 57
Paine, Sylvia, 56–58, 121
pilgrimage, xi, xvi, 94, 95, 100, 110
playing jump-rope, 30
poetry, 7, 9, 12, 39, 98, 107, 115
poor, care for the, 25, 28, 39
portraits, 105
prayer, 4, 14, 20, 22, 35, 36, 46, 52, 53, 62, 67, 68, 70, 72, 82,
    88, 89, 91, 92, 94, 111

Qannád, Áqá Riḍá, 28
Qazvíní, Javád-i-, 12
Qur'án, 61

Randall, Ruth, 46, 120
Randall, William Henry, 47, 120
Randall Winckler, Bahíyyih, 44–51, 80–82, 100–102, 120
Revelation, witnessing of, 4, 6–7
rosewater, 4, 7, 12, 13, 42, 46, 51, 52, 82, 86, 91, 100

Samandarí, Ṭaráẓulláh, vii, 8–16, 116
school, 24, 25, 30, 32, 68–69, 71, 73, 74, 75
Schopflocher, Siegfried, 110
service, 48
Shoghi Effendi, xv, 30, 31, 42, 45, 47, 48, 51, 59–95, 110, 111
singing, 39
studies, 18, 70
    Arabic, 24
    Bahá'í Writings, 24
    calligraphy, 19, 23–25
    carpentry, 24
    cleanliness, 26
    conduct, 26
    English, 23, 24, 26
    French, 71
    mathematics, 24
    Persian, 23, 24
    reading, 23
    shoemaking, 24
    tailoring, 24
    trade and vocation, 24

Tablets, 3, 4, 7, 10, 19, 29, 42, 51, 56, 63, 72, 80, 82, 86, 91, 109
Tabrízí, Áqá Muḥammad-i-, 5, 114
teaching, 7, 97
theatricals, 74
thrift, 77
True, Arna, 29–30, 117
True, Corrine, 29

Ustád Muḥammad-‘Alí, 9

Varqá, ‘Alí Muḥammad, 5, 114
Varqá, ‘Azíz ‘Azízu’lláh, 5–7, 114
Varqá, Rúḥu’lláh, 7–8, 115

Yazdí, ‘Alí, 41–44, 120
Yazdí, ‘Azíz, 51–56, 120

Zaynu’l-Muqarrabín, 24